Poverty in World Hi:

MW00466914

Poverty is a perennial problem in world history, but over time its causes have shifted from local issues like natural disasters or warfare to more global economic issues which impact on available resources, systems of distribution and potential solutions. *Poverty in World History* focuses upon the period from around 1500 onward when poverty became a global issue, and uses the process of globalization as the chief lens through which to study and understand poverty in world history.

The result is both a tying together of significant strands of world history and an examination of changing attitudes toward poverty and poor relief throughout the world. This wide-ranging study underscores a major consequence of increased cultural and economic interaction among the world's societies, highlighting the similarities and differences in impacts and responses to the resulting smaller globe. Topics include:

- Innovations in early modern poor relief
- The causes of trends toward a globalization of poverty after 1500
- Poor relief from 1945 to the present
- Poverty, morality and the state

A genuinely global survey of world poverty from 1500 to the present day, *Poverty in World History* is essential reading for students of world history.

Steven M. Beaudoin is currently Associate Professor of History at Centre College, Kentucky. He recently edited *The Industrial Revolution*, a reader for Houghton Mifflin's 'Problems in European Civilization' series. His research focuses on charity and civil society in nineteenth-century Europe, and the rise of the European welfare state.

Themes in World History
Series editor: Peter N. Stearns

The *Themes in World History* series offers focused treatment of a range of human experiences and institutions in the world history context. The purpose is to provide serious, if brief, discussions of important topics as additions to textbook coverage and document collections. The treatments will allow students to probe particular facets of the human story in greater depth than textbook coverage allows, and to gain a fuller sense of historians' analytical methods and debates in the process. Each topic is handled over time – allowing discussions of changes and continuities. Each topic is assessed in terms of a range of different societies and religions – allowing comparisons of relevant similarities and differences. Each book in the series helps readers deal with world history in action, evaluating global contexts as they work through some of the key components of human society and human life.

Gender in World History
Peter N. Stearns

**Consumerism in World History:
The Global Transformation of
Desire**
Peter N. Stearns

Warfare in World History
Michael S. Neiberg

**Disease and Medicine in World
History**
Sheldon Watts

**Western Civilization in World
History**
Peter N. Stearns

**The Indian Ocean in World
History**
Milo Kearney

**Asian Democracy in World
History**
Alan T. Wood

Revolutions in World History
Michael D. Richards

Migration in World History
Patrick Manning

Sports in World History
David G. McComb

**The United States in World
History**
Edward J. Davies II

Food in World History
Jeffrey M. Pilcher

Alcohol in World History
Gina Hames

Childhood in World History
Peter N. Stearns

Religion in World History
John Super and Briane Turley

Poverty in World History

Steven M. Beaudoin

Routledge
Taylor & Francis Group

LONDON AND NEW YORK

First published 2007
by Routledge
2 Park Square, Milton Park, Abingdon, Oxon OX14 4RN

Simultaneously published in the USA and Canada
by Routledge
270 Madison Avenue, New York, NY 10016

Routledge is an imprint of the Taylor & Francis Group, an informa business

© 2007 Steven M. Beaudoin

Typeset in Garamond by Taylor & Francis Books
Printed and bound in Great Britain by TJ International Ltd, Padstow, Cornwall

British Library Cataloguing in Publication Data
A catalogue record for this book is available from the British Library

Library of Congress Cataloging in Publication Data
Beaudoin, Steven M. (Steven Maurice), 1965–
Poverty in world history / Steven M. Beaudoin.
p. cm. – (Themes in world history)
Includes index.
1. Poverty – History. 2. Public welfare. 3. Economic assistance. I. Title. II. Series.
HC79.P6B375 2007
362.509 – dc22
2006019048

ISBN10: 0-415-25459-0   ISBN13: 978-0-415-25459-5 (pbk)
ISBN10: 0-415-25458-2   ISBN13: 978-0-415-25458-8 (hbk)
ISBN10: 0-203-96645-7   ISBN13: 978-0-203-96645-7 (ebk)

Contents

Acknowledgements   vi

Introduction   1

1   Poverty and charity in the pre-modern world: 15
    causes, perceptions, and strategies

2   Poverty in the emerging global economy   35

3   Innovations in early modern poor relief   48

4   Industrialization, imperialism, and world poverty,   57
    1750–1945

5   Poverty, morality, and the state, 1750–1945   77

6   Poverty and poor relief after 1945   94

    Conclusion   113

    Index   119

Acknowledgements

Anyone who has studied poverty cannot help but be struck by the importance of family and community as enduring resources for those in need. For the historian of poverty, that support network is no less important. My thanks, therefore, to Peter N. Stearns and Gina Hames, who were instrumental in the very inception of this book.

Closer to home, Rick Axtell, Mary Daniels, Helen Emmitt, and Lori Hartmann-Mahmud made this a much stronger work by reading more drafts than any of them would care to remember. I could not have completed this without their help. For its part, Centre College supported me with a sabbatical and Faculty Development funds that allowed me to benefit from the thoughtful and valuable research assistance of Samantha White and Lindsay Yeakel. At Routledge, Victoria Peters graciously accepted delays, while Emma Langley skillfully guided the manuscript through its final stages. Finally, my family has always been a crucial source of care and support for everything I have done. This book is dedicated to them: my parents, Pete and Jeannine Beaudoin, and my partner, John Rusnak.

Introduction

In 2001, in Mascarenha, Mozambique, only one ambulance served a population of more than 500,000. In the district's medical center, while one nurse assisted over eighty-five patients a day, another risked HIV contamination daily while washing their limited supply of used syringes. As for medication, the local pharmacist hadn't even stocked a vitamin since 1999. To increase the level of these services was simply impossible; it was too expensive. Things weren't much better in the rest of the country. Overall, three out of four people in this impoverished sub-Saharan African state lived on less than forty cents a day. Yet the central state could do little to help. Designated a "Heavily Indebted Poor Country" by the World Bank and the International Monetary Fund (IMF), Mozambique paid over $70 million annually in debt service. And Mozambique wasn't alone. In all, forty nations shared that unenviable qualifier at the dawn of the twenty-first century; together, these states owed over $212 billion! Added to the debts of those poor nations fortunate enough to escape the IMF's criteria for this classification, the total external debt of developing countries rose to over $2 trillion. As the village of Mascarenha demonstrates all too clearly, crippled by the high cost of debt service, these indebted states could offer few social programs, leaving many of their people to suffer from extreme want.

But poverty isn't simply a problem for developing countries like Mozambique. Even in industrialized nations, it remains a persistent affliction for millions, with rates of people living below the poverty line ranging between 10 percent and 15 percent. It's been almost forty years, for example, since President Lyndon Johnson created the Appalachian Regional Commission as part of his War on Poverty and, despite some impressive gains, little has improved for many in the region, which stretches from New York to Mississippi and incorporates nearly 23 million people. While the region's overall poverty rate has been halved since 1965, it still stands at 15 percent, with parts of rural central Appalachia like eastern Kentucky struggling under rates as high as 27 percent. In 2004, the joblessness in some areas reached 17 percent, comprising many who had simply given up and ceased even looking for employment. Moreover, in many regions, things are going to get worse before they get better, as local economies dependent on coal and tobacco expect significant downturns in the coming years. As one recent Commission report admitted, achievements in some areas have transformed the region from one of uniform poverty to one of striking contrasts, where relatively prosperous counties stand out among those that lack even basic infrastructure like water and sewer systems. And poverty isn't relegated to Appalachia alone. Studies now indicate that 1 in 5 children throughout the United States are born into poverty. Clearly, need and want have not been banished to the Third World.

According to a 1994 United Nations report, 1.1 billion of the world's people live in poverty – over 18 percent of the global population. Among them, poverty has many faces. It is the single mother of three in the United States who cannot find a job that pays more than the minimum wage; it is the Nigerian family that lives in squalor amid oil reserves that provide riches for only a very few of their compatriots; it is the Pakistani farmer contemplating the illegal opium trade as the only cash crop that can feed his children; it is the Brazilian boy who helps support his family with the money he earns doing odd jobs on the streets of Sao Paulo. A careful inspection of each of these and other cases reveals both startling similarities and striking differences. In many societies, the poor are predominately women and children, they have limited education, and they work at jobs that their cultures have defined as "low skilled." But the level of services to which they have recourse varies enormously, as does their overall place within society – what some scholars label their level of "social exclusion." Has this always been the case? Have the poor always been with us, as the saying goes? Have the causes of poverty changed over time? Have definitions of poverty remained constant? How have solutions to the misery of deprivation differed over time and among diverse societies?

This book focuses on these and other questions relating to the study of poverty in the context of world history. Why poverty and why world history? The answers are quite simple. As the evening news reports show us nightly, we have more than just a passing interest in understanding this fundamental characteristic of so many lives. Indeed, if, as the popular saying has it, money is the root of all evil, its absence can be traced to many of today's conflicts and tomorrow's calamities.[1] In places as diverse as Kosovo and Sudan, the scarcity of resources has fueled ethnic prejudices; in the streets of Cairo's slums and in the shadows of now-idle East German factories, intolerance is growing in the guise of militant religious fundamentalism and neo-Nazism; in the Brazilian Amazon, rainforests are denuded and indigenous cultures destroyed in the scramble for more fertile farmland. Closer to home, researchers have demonstrated a link between poverty and the social stresses that generate high crime, divorce, and alcohol/drug abuse rates. Each of these problems can be directly or indirectly tied to the hopelessness, misery, and desperation that follow in poverty's wake. At the same time, different solutions have met with varying rates of success. After more than $3.7 billion of its foreign debt was forgiven, Mozambique increased its spending on health and education by over $20 million between 1996 and 1999. In fact, Mozambique is frequently cited as a success story in sub-Saharan Africa largely because of the peaceful resolution of its civil war – a significant cause of poverty in many countries. Still, healthcare throughout much of the nation remains scarce. In industrialized countries, too, governments propose job programs and welfare reform, but impoverishment persists. Despite over a decade of record prosperity, recent studies reveal that the number of children living in poverty in the United States is currently rising. Against the backdrop of amazing wealth generated in the world over the last century, these examples of need and want, as well as the absence of lasting and comprehensive solutions, are exasperating. As with any problem, only a thorough understanding of its root causes, varied manifestations, and the complex reactions it engenders can form the foundation for those solutions.

Yet for many of us, our knowledge and comprehension rests solely on what we hear and read in the media, the most common source for information today. All too often the news stories that form the core of our perceptions distort or over-simplify reality. For example, television images of starving children in Ethiopia and Somalia, flashed before American and European viewers sitting comfortably in their own living rooms, were essential to a subsequent outpouring of aid during the 1980s and 1990s. At the same time, the term "welfare queen," a woman who is willing to have more children to increase the amount of government assistance she receives each month, also entered the American lexicon. Both images, supported by the media, achieved their desired responses, increased aid and welfare reform respectively. But they also obscured a fuller appreciation of the causes and nature of poverty in each setting, as well as the most effective solutions. For the most part, these sources tell us very little about poverty and the poor. Even well intentioned publications and broadcasts do not have the space to introduce the complexities that characterize world poverty. Those who suffer from poverty can find little lasting assistance if our awareness rests only on the images of starving Ethiopian children and "welfare queens."

This book represents a first step in the journey toward a deeper understanding of poverty. It does not purport to offer new solutions, but to present the state of current scholarship, establishing a foundation for further thought, research, and hopefully action. And that scholarship is growing. The topic is not only timely, but it also lies at the heart of many of the themes central to history, economics, world politics, and even religion. In history, for instance, poverty and the varied attempts to alleviate it lie at the nexus of social, cultural, economic, and political history, drawing together such topics as gender relations, kin networks, commodity exchange, and state development. It also relates to the rise and changing nature of the international economy, the growth of religious movements like liberation theology and Islamic fundamentalism, and the evolving roles of states and non-governmental organizations. Resting at such an important crossroads, this book brings together works from many different disciplines, from anthropology to economics, and presents the various approaches to this complex subject. The result is not a partisan treatise. Rather, the goal is to provide the reader with a general literacy of a problem that will only grow in importance in the coming decades.

Defining poverty

But how exactly are we to define this problem? And how should we measure its extent? Experts disagree. There are roughly three approaches to these central issues, each with its own merits and drawbacks. At its most basic level, poverty can be described as complete destitution – absolute poverty, sometimes called extreme poverty, is the lack of the basic elements needed for human survival: food, water, proper clothing, and shelter. Scholars have based this minimum level on either caloric intake or, more commonly, on the cost of maintaining proper nutrition. To a certain extent, this is the American approach. The US government establishes its poverty line using the Orshansky scale, named for Molly Orshansky, the Social Security Administration economist who designed it in 1963. This scale uses the minimum expenses needed to maintain proper nutrition and then augments this with other costs considered vital (it's in these additional costs that the US system moves beyond an "absolute" definition of poverty). Of course, the prices for these essentials may vary enormously in diverse parts of the globe, complicating cross-cultural assessments of poverty. For this reason, researchers frequently use "PPP dollars" or "purchasing power parity dollars" to measure consumption. The PPP dollar reflects the purchasing power of a currency – the amount it would cost in each currency for similar goods and services throughout the world. This makes it possible to establish the bare minimum for survival in different societies. According to the World Bank, the absolute poverty line in the developing world is 1 PPP$ a day (in 1985 purchasing power parity dollars).

For many researchers, however, the problems posed by this definition and these measurements outweigh their usefulness. First, basing a measurement of poverty primarily upon nutritional requirements glosses over factors like seasonal fluctuations in food supply and cost, as well as cultural dictates on consumption and food preparation. This is complicated by the fact that this technique takes a "snap-shot" view of poverty and society; it determines a level of poverty without understanding some of its fundamental causes. It overlooks, for example, the connections between impoverishment and the life-cycle (i.e. when impoverishment is particularly linked to old age, child-hood, and/or marital status) and thus ignores a central characteristic of poverty in many societies. Second, it makes it difficult to factor in things that are essential to survival but are not part of private budgets, such as clean water and sanitation. Third, this approach privileges actual poverty over potential poverty, discounting the millions whose precarious situation gives them enough today, but leaves tomorrow insecure. Finally, for the vast majority of the world's poor, absolute poverty fails to capture their situation. Thanks in large part to the "green revolution" and improved transportation, relatively few (in global terms) risk starvation, even though they are vulnerable in many other ways. Maintaining such a narrow definition ignores their plight.

Most scholars have opted instead for the concept of relative poverty, or overall poverty, a definition that moves beyond the question of survival to incorporate accessibility to what society as a whole values. Focusing more on living standards, like hot and cold running water, access to healthcare, and disposable income, relative poverty shifts the spotlight from minimums to averages, both within individual communities and countries, and among the other nations of the world as well. In this approach, need and want are defined contextually, based on a given population's wealth and, to a certain extent, ideals. The major tool for assessing relative poverty remains income, although researchers also include statistics on sanitation, medical facilities, housing, etc. In any given country, then, scholars determine impoverishment by relating a person's disposable income (income above that required for survival) to the national average. For international comparisons, most use the gross national product (GNP) per capita. The GNP represents the total sum of the goods and services produced by a national economy (the GDP, or gross domestic product) plus the income residents receive from abroad (minus the same income produced by foreigners working within that country). This method has gained widespread appeal because it avoids many of the problems associated with the absolute poverty approach. For this reason, the World Bank has established the poverty line in industrialized nations at 14.40 PPP\$ a day, substantially higher than the 1 PPP\$ a day level for developing countries.

Like absolute poverty, this definition has its critics, particularly those who question the overwhelming reliance on income and consumption as measurement tools. Concerns arise immediately, for example, over the basic unit of income assessment, the household or the individual. Opting for a household calculation risks underestimating the number of women and children who suffer from poverty; larger families tend to be poorer with income shared more widely, and income distribution within the family may be far from equal. Using the GNP per capita to aggregate to the individual allows researchers to capture differences within families, but it, too, is not without its problems. First, the GNP per capita represents an average; gauging poverty on all incomes calculated from overall production doesn't take into account the vast variations possible in income distribution. Using the incomes of people like Bill Gates and Richard Branson to calculate average incomes hardly seems appropriate; it's even less appropriate in nations where a wide gulf exists between impoverished masses and an extremely wealthy but small elite. Second, GNP per capita ignores the impact of what is still a basic unit of society throughout much of the world. A household may bring certain resources to bear on poverty that the individual alone does not enjoy. Measuring poverty along lines of per capita income and not potential assets, from material possessions to social relations, overlooks this. Third, assessing poverty on private income or consumption alone is, for many, too limiting. To what extent should public spending on healthcare and sanitation be incorporated into poverty calculations? Such considerations may seem irrelevant to measuring poverty in Western Europe, but are fundamental to understanding it in Mozambique. Finally, income isn't as sensitive to social and cultural differences as many scholars would prefer. Determining luxury from necessity, for example, is fraught with difficulty. Is a car a luxury? Perhaps in areas with good public transportation, but even in the US, where public transportation is lacking and urban sprawl is common, labeling it a luxury raises real problems with significant consequences for determining disposable income. Income measurements also ignore the cultural dimensions of poverty, which often entail a certain social stigma and state of mind in some countries that is lacking in others. All of these considerations render poverty far more complex than income measurements can reveal.

To overcome these problems, and expand a definition that they feel is too constraining, some researchers advance a third definition, often referred to as a human capabilities approach. Poverty, according to this view, is the absence of choice. In some respects, this is a marriage of both absolute and relative definitions of poverty. It recognizes an absolute nature to impoverishment, but sets the defining element at the optimum, not minimum, standard of living; at the same time, it requires that such optimums be determined in relation to specific cultural and social values that differ according to environment. Poverty is thus much more than just a dearth of material goods. It is the inability to participate actively in life, from attaining the educational levels that optimize career choices, to acquiring both time and income to engage in various common leisure activities. It is also the absence of political freedom, personal security, dignity, and self respect. It is these intangibles in particular that give this definition a culturally determined characteristic. In the end, poverty cannot be defined objectively; it is based on a society's ideals and norms. This approach has led some scholars to argue that poverty, by its very nature, can never be eradicated. It will always exist because it is a necessary tool for establishing standards – there must always be those who fall below certain benchmarks to valorize those criteria. That doesn't mean, however, that impoverishment cannot be assessed and alleviated. To do this, scholars have added a host of new measurements, from school enrollments, to crime rates, to long-term unemployment.

But casting the net so widely, acknowledging the many intangibles that go into a rich, fulfilling life, produces a number of questions and concerns. How exactly should aid workers assist the poor? Are there absolutes to personal security, to self-respect? Can and should one society dictate to another how to provide political freedom and dignity to all of its citizens? This is a particularly thorny question when it comes to women and children. Are the restrictions on women in certain Islamic cultures a form of impoverishment? Similar concerns reflect more common reservations over measurement. How does one measure levels of choice and security?

There is no easy solution to these problems of meaning and magnitude, or to those yielded by the other definitions and measurements. Perhaps the best path, and the one this book follows, is to acknowledge the benefits and drawbacks of each, drawing upon them when appropriate and noting the levels of poverty that each designates. This enables researchers to arrive at a composite, all-inclusive yet clearly nuanced picture of world poverty. To a certain extent, this is the World Bank's approach, designating different levels of absolute poverty in developing and industrialized nations. But this still privileges income and consumption. A broader approach includes such data as rates of literacy, school enrollment, life expectancy, infant mortality, and unemployment. The Physical Quality of Life Index (PQLI), for example, focuses on what its creator David Morris terms "real life chances" by measuring infant mortality, life expectancy at the age of one, and basic literacy.

Going even further, the United Nations Development Programme (UNDP) uses complex formulae to calculate indices for both Human Development and Human Poverty. The former, adopting a capabilities approach, measures factors that contribute to personal fulfillment and opportunity broadly defined; the latter concentrates on the extent of deprivation within the community. The Human Development Index (HDI) is determined using data on life expectancy at birth, educational attainment (a combination of adult literacy and educational enrollment ratios), and income. In order to attain a basis for comparison, the UNDP also incorporates fixed maximum and minimum values for all variables. For example, it calculates the index for life expectancy as follows: Index = (actual value − minimum value)/(maximum value − actual value). Moreover, the formula for rating real income per capita is derived from a maximum of less than 6,000 PPP\$, the world average income in 1995, and discounts any income that surpasses this. The overall HDI is the average of the life expectancy index, educational attainment index, and adjusted real GDP per capita index. For the Poverty Index, or HPI, which shifts emphasis away from capabilities to levels of deprivation, the UNDP goes even further to manage the variations among different nations; it has created two formulae, one for developing nations and another for industrialized countries. For developing countries, researchers take into account the percentage of the population expected to die before the age of forty, the percentage of illiterate adults, the percentage without access to clean water and health services, and the percentage of underweight children under five. For industrialized nations, where access to clean water and health services are much more secure, the formula's variables include the percentage of the population not expected to survive to sixty, the percentage of adults who are functionally illiterate, the percentage of people living below an income poverty line of 50 percent of the median disposable income, and the rate of long-term unemployment. Scholars use this last figure, the rate of long-term unemployment, as a measurement for social inclusion, arguing that after twelve months of unemployment one no longer has the means, or the appearance, of being an active member of society.

Together, the HDI and HPI offer a much more comprehensive and nuanced evaluation of poverty in the world today than the measurement of income alone. They assess both the potential for a healthy, successful life in a given society, and the extent and nature of poverty among those for whom such potential remains out of reach. The results can be quite surprising. In the Arab states, for example, income poverty (i.e. the percentage of people below the 1 PPP$-a-day poverty line) stands at a remarkable 4 percent, but human poverty (as reflected in the HPI) remains relatively high at 32 percent, indicating that rising aggregate income has not translated into increased opportunity and choice for large segments of the population. Taken together, the range of numbers offers a much more thorough assessment of poverty. Egypt, for instance, with an HPI of 34.8 in 1997, ranked 44th among the 78 developing countries ranked by the UNDP; 30th according to the HDI, and 31st according to the 1 PPP$-a-day poverty line. In other words, while approximately 20 percent of Egyptians could be defined as income-poor, almost 35 percent remained impoverished in terms of potential and choice, lacking adequate access to education and healthcare. The higher HDI rank suggests, moreover, that such impoverishment exists amid substantial income disparity; the possibilities for human development exist more widely than they are shared throughout society. Such figures are particularly valuable in policy analysis, for they point out when development programs should become more "pro-poor" (i.e. when they should be aimed at alleviating misery among the most needy) and when they should be more widespread and available to the population as a whole. The results thus give us a much more complete understanding of global poverty in today's world. Achieving the same insight for the past is considerably more difficult, however.

Poverty and history

Of course, the UNDP's methods aren't without their problems. For example, it would like to measure social exclusion among developing nations too, but it recognizes that reliable data on this is difficult to come by in those countries.

Indeed, all of these definitions and measurements are dependent upon reliable data. While this is a serious problem for researchers of contemporary need, it is even worse for historians of poverty. First of all, the poor themselves usually leave no records. Unlike researchers today, historians cannot go out into the field to observe and survey. Second, historians must also contend with the inescapable problem of all of our sources: bias. The documents left behind all, to a certain extent, reflect the ideals of the group that wrote them and then chose to preserve them. Returning to our earlier examples of Ethiopian children and welfare queens, we can readily see the dangers inherent in relying on such images as sources for understanding poverty. Often this can be accommodated by gathering as many sources as possible, from perspectives as diverse as possible. For historians of poverty, this list includes graphic imagery like art and photography; letters, journals, and other documents from the poor and aid workers; newspaper investigations; government data; and academic treatises. Of course, this full range does not exist for all historical periods. In fact, the vast majority of these sources date primarily from the modern period, particularly after the nineteenth century, when the West, which dominated most of the world, took an active interest in documenting, explaining, and alleviating poverty. But, as these documents become more plentiful, their bias becomes even stronger. Virtually all of their authors wrote with the conscious desire to sway opinion. They can be read easily for attitudes toward poverty and the poor, but with much greater difficulty for what they say about the poor themselves and their lives, including unofficial strategies for dealing with want and need.

Recognizing these difficulties allows historians to avoid their shortcomings, but it brings them no closer to a workable and meaningful definition of poverty or a technique for measuring it in the past. Consequently, many adopt the definitions and standards evident in their documents, while noting that these reflect the attitudes of society's "haves," not the "have-nots." Indeed, attitudes toward poverty and the poor often make up the lion's share of most histories of poverty. And accepting contemporary views makes a great deal of sense. After all, according to these historians, it is almost meaningless to single out a "laboring poor" (those who make enough to survive but risk poverty at the first accident, bad harvest, or large expense), when up until the twentieth century, that condition described the majority of the world's population. Similarly, one can question the merits of defining poverty as the absence of choice in a plantation society marked by widespread slavery. Yet there is value to keeping today's standards in sight while casting our gaze back to the past. Like the UNDP's formulae, maintaining a wide definition of poverty permits the historian to distinguish levels of need. While acknowledging that contemporaries may not have viewed certain conditions as characteristic of poverty (white slave-owners, for example, did not view slaves as poor), studying all forms of need and want offers a more comprehensive approach to both poverty and the societies that confronted it. In other words, we must adopt a view of poverty that allows considerable flexibility and can take into account all types of conditions, not just those that contemporaries labeled poor.

In this book, then, the poor are divided into three categories depending upon the nature and root cause of their impoverishment. At the heart of this system of classification is the view that all poverty is born of insecurity, and it is by focusing principally on that situation rather than on particular meanings that we learn the most about need and hardship. Emphasizing economic considerations over broader concerns like political freedom and personal security, these categories still allow for significant evolution over time and for diversity. Each category rests on the roots of vulnerability to poverty, regardless of how a given civilization might define it. Individuals in the first category, the "destitute," lack the capacity to survive without assistance; their insecurity is total. Throughout most of world history, they have been the orphaned, handicapped, and elderly, and it is this group that has traditionally attracted the greatest attention in systems of poor relief and charity. The second group, the "structural" poor, comprises those who have the ability to meet their own needs, be it survival or active engagement in society, but not the means. Traditionally, this incorporates men and women who lacked resources like land and/or access to paid employment, the "able-bodied poor." In today's more affluent nations, however, those without adequate education have joined their ranks, for they lack the tools necessary to active engagement in an information-based economy. For the structural poor, then, insecurity is a product of the economy's structure; it is contingent on a society's system of resource allocation. The "conjunctural" poor, the third group, consist of those who are capable of meeting their own needs because of their access to resources, but who remain vulnerable because they cannot insulate themselves from misfortune. They live with the knowledge that economic downturns, illness, and life-cycle changes can put pressure on limited budgets and tip the balance in poverty's favor, but such impoverishment is typically a temporary condition. When the "inability to survive" best described poverty, these people feared hunger; where it is now characterized by a below-average standard of living, they fear an inability to provide for their children what other families enjoy. (While some scholars add a fourth category – the "crisis" poor, those who fall into need because of a collective catastrophe, like famine and warfare – in this study they are a subgroup of the conjunctural poor, for their poverty is also temporary, even if their resources typically allow them to withstand economic fluctuations and short-term personal adversity, but not economic calamity.) In each case, whether poverty is defined as the inability to meet basic needs, an inferior standard of living in relation to social norms, or the absence of choice, the poor all suffer from a similar condition, a certain precariousness that could result in penury. It is the root causes of that misery and the possibilities for reversing impoverishment that distinguishes one group from the other.

The chapters that follow thus explore the causes and extent of poverty as captured in these three categories, with the goal of understanding why some causes have been more or less prevalent and how many people suffered from the various forms of vulnerability during certain periods and in individual societies. Discussion will focus both on obvious causes like famine and economic downturns, and on core origins like the nature of the economy and systems of resource allocation. As to extent, particular attention will go to assessing poverty's duration and distribution in various places and at different times, from long-term and widespread, to cyclical and individual or concentrated. At the same time, contemporary attitudes are not irrelevant. These determined the various measures people benefited from in their search for security, from official aid when they met the prevailing criteria of the day, to informal strategies when they did not, to some mixture of the two. Understanding how and why these definitions changed is also essential to the study of poverty in the past. In essence, this approach acknowledges the cultural variability of poverty by including contemporary attitudes, but without neglecting those who fell outside its parameters.

With an approach to discerning and investigating poverty firmly in place, this study requires one last element, a means for organizing and presenting the relevant data. When confronted with the history of something as complex and pervasive as need and want, historians face the choice of what some scholars have labeled a "lens" – a category of analysis, a perspective that allows the historian to find meaning in the past. On its own, the past has little sense, it is like raw data. The historian's task is to organize those data – those names, dates, and figures that make up past experiences – into something that has meaning, something from which we can draw lessons and a greater understanding of who we are and who we have been. That organization is the heart of the historian's argument, or interpretation; it is what allows two historians using the same data to draw very different conclusions. That doesn't mean, of course, that the historian can simply choose any lens she wants; historians have evidentiary standards that dictate which lenses have merit and which do not. Our analyses, submitted to the review of our peers, must meet certain requirements. They must incorporate all pertinent sources, while acknowledging their limitations; rest on a foundation of objectivity, within the limits of the possible; and effectively draw on the sources to form a well reasoned, defensible argument. With the history of poverty, there are many possible lenses. Gender, for example, offers a strong possibility. Current scholarship, after all, demonstrates that the world's poor are disproportionately female. Choosing gender as a lens, the historian would analyze the nature of the link between gender and poverty over time – i.e. Is gender a cause of poverty? Has it always been? How have different societies justified that link?

Without ignoring the intriguing question of gender, this study focuses primarily upon the process of globalization that began around the year 1500 AD as the chief lens through which to study and understand poverty in world history. Choosing globalization enhances our understanding of both poverty and world history itself precisely because poverty has been so closely tied to the process of globalization. Throughout much of the world before 1500, poverty resulted principally from local sources like natural disaster, warfare, and civilization-specific systems of distribution; few were affected by what were still regional trade networks. At the same time, most cultures viewed impoverishment as a natural part of life, rarely defined as the absence of material possessions. In Western Europe during the Middle Ages, for example, the term "poverty" frequently denoted spiritual impoverishment. After 1500, however, two trends began to emerge. First, as more people found themselves directly and indirectly reliant on world trade, poverty itself became more firmly fixed in the dynamics of that economy. As time passed, the world economy came to play a much greater causal role in world poverty, influencing both available resources and systems of distribution. This only intensified after the Second World War, as the Cold War and an expanding world economy involved more and more nations. Second, throughout much of the globe, different cultures adopted an evolving Western approach to destitution that defined it first and foremost as a lack of certain goods, a social challenge that required concerted action to reverse. Insecurity and want were no longer seen as natural, but as "problems" that demanded solutions. In addition, solutions, too, took on a global appearance, with public and private aid agencies enlarging their fields of action, culminating in the creation of such organizations as UNICEF and the World Bank. Currently, few scholars conceptualize poverty without some recognition of the world economy, and it remains defined chiefly along Western lines of material deprivation. The history of poverty, analyzed through the lens of globalization, thus ties together significant strands of world history. It underscores a major consequence of increased cultural and economic interaction among the world's societies, highlighting the similarities and differences in impacts and responses to the "smaller" globe that has resulted.

The remainder of this study, then, focuses primarily upon world history after 1500. To set a foundation, however, the first chapter comprises an examination of poverty before that date. It examines the causes of poverty in different civilizations, the ways those societies justified such misery, and their various approaches to its alleviation. This ranges from the almsgiving so central to many of the world's religions, like Islam, to the creation of early state institutions to prevent famine, like the vast imperial granaries of China. This chapter will provide a basis for assessing later developments as global conditions began to change in the sixteenth century. The next two chapters trace the evolution of poverty in the emerging Western-dominated world economy up to approximately 1750, when Europe began to industrialize. During this period, virtually all of the world's societies underwent some transformation as a result of Latin America's integration into the world economy. This included not only the detrimental impacts of Western trade on Latin America, but also the devastating inflation resulting from the influx of New World silver into China. Chapter 2 examines the rise of this world economy, its characteristics, and its impact on the world's civilizations, while Chapter 3 focuses on the responses such transformations provoked. Chapters 5 and 6 present a similar pairing for a different period in world history, the centuries ushered in by the West's industrialization, from 1750 to 1945. During this these years, the heyday of Western imperialism, the West succeeded in not only controlling the world economy, but also in shaping the internal economies of various societies to suit its purposes. India's textile industry, for example, was decimated to protect its British rival. At the same time, other societies began their own processes of industrialization in order to maintain their independence. Therefore, Chapter 4 examines industrialization's impact on poverty not only in the West, but also as it began its spread to Russia and Japan. It also includes coverage of those areas of the world economy where poverty rose due to colonization, like India and sub-Saharan Africa, and competition with the West, including China and the Middle East. Chapter 5 details the rise of new "scientific" approaches to understanding poverty and new institutions that fall under the more general rubric of the welfare state. Of primary significance is the growing concept of the right to assistance. Finally, Chapter 6 focuses on world poverty as it has developed since 1945, when the West's relative decline became more pronounced in the face of decolonization, increased Soviet and Asian competition, and the continued spread of industrialization. The topics in this chapter include the importance of sustainable economic development as a means of eradicating poverty and the growth of international organizations of assistance and self-help to accomplish that goal.

One final note on the nature of this book and its organization: because it is based on the literature that already exists, this book has been guided more by what scholars have done than the questions that drive our interests in poverty. For this reason, these chapters are weighted in two directions. First, much of the research on poverty before the twentieth century focuses on Western Europe. Second, the available sources have also dictated that most of the literature concerns the more recent years. So, our view widens and deepens the closer we get to our own times. This is reflected in the chapters that follow. While every attempt is made to maintain a global focus, most of the cases reflect the more advanced state of the literature on poverty in Western history and on global poverty since 1945. Most of the material for poverty outside of the West before the Second World War can be gleaned from more general economic and social histories of the world's civilizations. But the absence of more specialized literature means that the chapters on poverty before 1945 are more weighted to the European and American experience, and the book pays more attention to the experiences of the poor since the nineteenth and twentieth centuries. Similarly, the sources for gauging poverty's extent are particularly rare and inconclusive for all but the most recent years. In Europe, some cities maintained irregular censuses of the poor before more accurate records became a hallmark of the nineteenth-century state, but these reflected contemporary attitudes, not true numbers of those in need. Historians also have the rolls of those who accepted municipal relief, but these do not indicate the numbers who requested assistance and received none. For these lacunae there is no easy solution. We must content ourselves with generalizations and impressions until data become more plentiful. As a result, the sections in this book devoted to the extent of poverty become more detailed in the chapters concerning the nineteenth and twentieth centuries. Before then, "snapshot" images, with their defects and limitations, remain our only option.

Further reading

On measuring poverty and human development: John Dixon and David Macarov (eds) *Poverty* (New York: Routledge, 1998); John Iliffe, *The African Poor* (New York: Cambridge University Press, 1987); UNDP, *Human Development Report* (New York: Oxford University Press, 1990–); Amartya Sen, *Poverty and Famines* (New York: Oxford University Press, 1982).

Chapter 1

Poverty and charity in the pre-modern world

Causes, perceptions, and strategies

Embarking on any study of poverty in the pre-modern world is challenging. First, historians have relatively few sources upon which to base their investigations. In many of the world's societies, statistics, like the concept of material poverty itself, is a relatively new idea. This, unfortunately, limits the detail and depth of our understanding; the farther back in time we search, the more tentative our conclusions must be. With few exceptions, most scholars must content themselves with studying broad, sweeping causes without achieving clear indications of the scope and extent of poverty within given societies. Conditions improve only slightly when the focus shifts to the various explanations and strategies that each community devised in the face of need and want. Elites, and the states they served, were far more interested in detailing their own actions and thoughts, particularly if these reflected well on their sense of generosity and piety. But even given their limitations, the written records are spotty and reflect the attitudes of only a small minority of the world's pre-modern population; rarely do they indicate how the majority lived and experienced hardship. Second, beyond the source deficiencies, the study of poverty in the pre-modern world is complicated by significant diversity. Before the sixteenth century, both the causes of poverty and the reactions it inspired were primarily rooted in the internal dynamics of individual civilizations and their immediate surroundings. The fledgling, far-flung networks of trade that joined the Afro-Eurasian landmass together into one "world" system were weak and had little impact upon how most of the world's societies functioned, let alone how their people lived their lives. As a result, the history of poverty during these centuries must be sought in the different socioeconomic, cultural, and political contexts that emerged in each civilization, especially their systems of resource allocation and their religious precepts and institutions.

Luckily, the number of historians willing to grapple with such difficulties has grown remarkably over the last decades. Based on their efforts, this chapter sets our study's foundation by examining the nature and causes of poverty in the pre-modern world, the various means by which different cultures perceived such need, and the various strategies both individuals and societies devised to cope with it. For the vast majority of the pre-modern world's population, poverty meant hunger, and almost no one was free from its specter. Yet the specific causes for both structural and conjunctural poverty could shift from region to region, depending in particular on the resources that shaped economic life. Similarly, given limitations on resources, a great deal of attention in many societies went into determining who should receive aid, but the qualities that made these men and women "deserving" depended upon diverse cultural values. Finally, while those who suffered deprivation might seek assistance from the same types of sources – institutions designed to help the needy; private and unofficial charity; family; and informal strategies devised by the poor themselves – the avail-ability of each type differed across time and space. In short, the perceptions of need and want – and the possibilities for relief – were based on funda-mental assumptions about resources and community specific to each culture. Establishing these differences, and their place within a broad set of common-alities, provides a framework for analyzing the impacts of the world economy as it developed after 1450 and for understanding the contexts in which new strategies were considered and implemented.

The nature and scope of poverty

In relation to poverty, the most basic similarity among all the world's pre-modern civilizations is that misery and insecurity remained inexorably linked to hunger. Regardless of the degree of commercial development, all of the world's sedentary societies were agricultural at their core. Moreover, despite impressive technological breakthroughs over the centuries, like the yoke, heavier metal plows, and faster growing strains of grain, the state of the world's technology before 1450 limited the supply of available food. Indeed, in the initial stages of civilization, changes in growing conditions could destroy entire societies, as was the case for ancient India's Harappan civilization in the Indus River Valley, which mysteriously disappeared around 1500 BCE. While earlier interpretations imagined waves of invaders, archeological evidence now suggests that alterations in the intensity of the southwest monsoon and its impact on Indus River flooding patterns may have had a greater impact in the Harappan decline. Without seasonal flooding along the Indus to replenish the soil and supply irrigation systems, much as the Nile did in Egypt, agricultural productivity fell off and a vibrant urban culture faded into obscurity. Although the classical civiliza-tions in China's rich Yellow and Yangtze River valleys, on the shores of the Mediterranean Sea, and along the banks of India's Ganges River escaped such fates, even their successors in the post-classical period could not produce vast surpluses of agricultural goods over long stretches of time. While historians continue to debate the exact relationship between technology, agricultural production, and population growth, one thing is clear: hunger remained a palpable fear throughout the pre-modern world. In this context, then, poverty can be defined best in absolute terms – it was the inability to sustain life, not the absence of material possessions.

At the same time, it is important to recognize and maintain the distinction between famine and food scarcity. Famine, the widespread decline in food availability for the community as a whole, is marked most by its duration and its sweeping impacts. Not one bad harvest, but a series of disastrous crop yields creates a famine. And, since it frequently results in elevated mortality rates and far-reaching societal responses like mass migration from one region to another, it also typically prompts large-scale measures to assist those afflicted. Food scarcity, on the other hand, is reflected in short-term inflation in food prices, which can be severe, but only for a portion of the population. It produces pockets of need, no less dire for those afflicted, but not widespread starvation. This, according to scholars, was commonplace in the pre-modern world. In ancient Athens, for example, one in every six years between 403 and 323 BCE were marked by food shortages, while that rate was one in every five years for Rome between 123 and 50 BCE. Similarly, in China, officials recorded agricultural disasters in 119 years between 25 and 220 CE, leaving only seventy-six years without shortages. Famine, in contrast, became a rarity as civilizations developed. Or, more precisely, it became a localized catastrophe, linked as much to the ineffective distribution of stores from neighboring areas as to the calamities that normally created such widespread dearth in the first place.

This means that chronic hunger and undernourishment, not starvation, was the most common form of poverty in the pre-modern world, and it could affect almost anyone. Given the limitations on agricultural surpluses, the vast majority of the world's population could easily slide into conjunctural poverty. They had the physical means to support themselves in optimal conditions (i.e. health, good weather, access to land and other resources, etc.), but rarely produced enough to withstand variations in their precarious living conditions. In good years, the meager surplus they produced helped provide for the destitute and structural poor, and the elite, those who might join the conjunctural poor if the crisis was severe and long in duration. The history of poverty is to be found, then, not just among the destitute and infirm, but also among the multitudes whose lives weaved back and forth across the line separating hunger and subsistence. Consequently, the search for poverty's causes must focus on three central concerns: (1) the conditions that could cause an individual or family to slide below subsistence; (2) the circumstances that could cause the number of people below that threshold to swell at particular moments in time; and (3) the economic structures that determined how many people remained susceptible to such a slide as a normal part of life.

Poverty's causes

Determining poverty's causes during the pre-modern period is least compli-cated at the two extremes: individual destitution and mass conjunctural poverty. For the destitute, the causes of impoverishment were the same throughout the various classical and post-classical civilizations – any misfor-tune that made it impossible for an individual to provide for him or herself. In some instances, this misfortune accompanied certain stages in the life cycle. Children and the elderly, for example, suffered from need unless someone provided assistance. That's why orphans were particularly at risk. Among adults in the most productive years of their lives, hunger struck those who lost their ability to care for themselves due to illness or handicap. It could also afflict a family whose chief breadwinner died, suffered from a disability, or sustained a serious injury that depleted the household's resources and precluded a return to usual earning power. It is impossible to estimate the rates of such poverty during this period, but since adequate medical care was scarce, one can assume that it was fairly high.

On a societal level, conjunctural or crisis poverty often resulted from natural or manmade calamities like floods, droughts, and warfare. Such disasters could destroy crops, prevent farmers from taking to the fields (especially in the case of warfare), or disrupt the distribution of food after harvest. Indeed, humankind learned early on that separating an enemy from supplies like fresh water was an effective tool in forcing others to submit. While we often associate such misery with sudden catastrophes, it is impor-tant to note that other more slowly evolving causes could contribute to such crises by diminishing available resources, as occurred in the Harappan civi-lization noted above. Salinization and siltation could threaten essential irrigation networks, while long-term alterations in climate might shorten the growing season. Scientists estimate, for instance, that ancient China experienced one such period of deterioration between the first and eighth centuries CE that reduced the growing season by 30–40 days. The result was chronic food shortage that swelled the ranks of the conjunctural poor. As with destitution, records that indicate the prevalence of such calamities was imprecise, but estimates lead historians to believe that food scarcity was a constant concern. In China alone, for instance, scholars have counted almost ninety agricultural disasters, from floods to hailstorms, from locusts to droughts, during the Eastern and Western Zhou dynasties, from 1027 to 221 BCE.

Recognizing the constant insecurity that might lead to destitution and widespread conjunctural poverty is only part of the search to understand the causes of poverty, however. It does not address the causes of two of the more common types of poverty: structural poverty – the misery that struck those who had the ability to meet their needs, but not the means, even in the best conditions for food production – and more limited forms of conjunctural poverty – impoverishment most often associated with less severe downturns in economic conditions. For that, the focus must shift away from the characteristics that all civilizations shared, like the insecurity produced by individual misfortune and climatic catastrophe, to the various systems of resource allocation adopted in each. According to Amartya Sen, a leading scholar of poverty and development, susceptibility to hunger is tied to the system of "entitlements" that structures a society. In other words, not everyone faces the possibility of starvation equally, and many factors can determine a person's risk, from geographic location and social standing, to sex and age. That susceptibility also changes over time. In early medieval Europe, for example, when market agriculture was in its infancy, famine and food shortages could be less severe for serfs because they were not dependent on systems of transportation for a steady supply of food and because their lords retained a certain responsibility for keeping them alive. City dwellers, on the other hand, were at the mercy of poorly maintained transportation networks. Moreover, within urban areas, to the extent that monetization had influenced the economy, those with a higher income could more readily afford food as famine drove up prices. As time passed and market economies evolved, however, the urban/rural split in entitlement shifted. Farmers who planted cash crops came to rely upon the same transportation networks as urban dwellers for sustenance. But, as those roads and canals developed, the routes connecting cities with one another became more secure, ensuring that well supplied cities in other regions could replenish the stocks of sister cities first. Only after urban officials could secure their own sources of food would they then permit newly restocked municipal granaries to be opened to residents outside their city walls. In other words, urban residents acquired a more secure entitlement to agricultural goods than peasants. Their needs were met first. A similar dynamic operated within households, where, in patriarchal cultures, adult men maintained a stronger entitlement than women and children.

Assessing susceptibility based on entitlement to resources – and subsequently the causes of structural and less severe conjunctural poverty – thus requires understanding the economic, political, and cultural structures that shaped particular societies. This is a difficult task for anyone seeking to understand the causes of poverty in the pre-modern world as a whole. It forces attention on the essential characteristics that most of the world's societies shared. Patriarchy, for example, made women more vulnerable to poverty than men throughout the world, even in societies where resources were plentiful; women in patriarchal societies had a difficult time maintaining any sort of individual claim to such resources. Widows and adult women who sought to live independently typically confronted male relatives who asserted their own claims to family property; those who resisted risked being squeezed by poverty until they conceded. Surrender meant subsistence, but subservience in an extended household.

Another significant shared characteristic was the prevalence of what one historian terms an "organic" economy, an economy based entirely on the productive capacity of land without benefit of any sources of energy beyond human and animal power.[1] In such economies, productivity is always constrained by the availability of land; as it becomes scarce, instances of structural and conjunctural poverty increase. This has inclined some scholars to argue that poverty truly originates with farming, even in areas with plentiful land. In hunting and gathering societies, resources were usually devoted to the entire group's survival. There was little strict social differentiation within the group to justify differences in entitlement. In agricultural societies, however, social distinctions became more common, with critical ramifications. As access to the fresh water necessary to agriculture grew in importance, the goal of production shifted from group to elite maintenance. The kings and temple keepers of ancient Sumeria in the Near East, for example, lived in societies organized around the production and extraction of agricultural surpluses earmarked for elite consumption. Although the health of the entire civilization depended upon supplying enough crops to those who grew them, elites commanded far greater shares of available resources than commoners. In short, agriculture led to hierarchies based in part on access to and control over land and fresh water, and this in turn led to poverty.

There is much of value in this interpretation, for excess appropriation was a frequent cause of food shortage among classical and post-classical civilizations, especially in militarized and urban societies like ancient Rome and China. In the Roman empire, for example, urban residents – typically citizens of the empire – maintained a stronger entitlement to resources than peasants. Even in years that witnessed a plentiful harvest, many peasants could face hunger. As the famous physician Galen, a resident of the urban outpost of Pergamum in the Asian stretches of the empire, noted in 148 CE:

> For those who live in the cities, in accordance with their habit of procuring sufficient grain at the beginning of the summer to last for the entire coming year, took from the fields all the wheat, barley, beans and lentils, leaving the other legumes to the *rustici*, although they even carted off no small portion of these to the city as well. Consequently the peasantry of these districts, having consumed during the winter whatever was left, were literally compelled for the rest of the year to feed on noxious plants, eating the shoots and tendrils of trees and shrubs, the bulbs and roots of unwholesome plants.

The state compounded such dearth by collecting taxes and manpower, which further decreased productivity. In China, during the Zhou and Qin dynasties, when population pressures were not yet great and migration to unsettled regions was still possible, some peasants chose to abandon their fields rather than submit to high taxes and conscription in armies or labor gangs, decreasing productivity and increasing the burdens on those left behind. In such instances, conjunctural poverty was the result for the remaining peasants; they had the ability and the means to provide for themselves, but outside forces stepped in to reduce their stores of available food.

Some argue, however, that hierarchy by itself does not lead to poverty; it only contributes to it when resources become scarce. That is why some scholars have emphasized the availability of resources, not just systems of allocation in determining poverty's causes. These historians make an important distinction between land-rich and land-scarce societies. In societies where land was plentiful and easily attained, structural poverty was virtually unknown. Subsistence agriculture dominated the economy, and able-bodied people could see to their own sustenance. The same holds true in non-agricultural economies, like the pastoral societies of sub-Saharan Africa and Central Asia, where physical hardship, a chief cause of destitution, was the primary cause of impoverishment. Conjunctural poverty, on the other hand, could be quite common in land-rich societies and was typically tied either to excess appropriation as described above or to the life-cycle of particular households. Young families with many mouths to feed but few grown children to contribute their labor to the household's survival, often experienced periods of impoverishment that would be alleviated once their older children could either work around the house or be hired out to other households.

In land-scarce societies, on the other hand, structural poverty was far more common and conjunctural poverty more pervasive. The increase in such impoverishment usually accompanied two other developments: overpopulation and the rise of commercial agriculture. The first factor follows from the argument that Thomas Malthus first articulated in the eighteenth century: population increases exponentially, while resources grow arithmetically; eventually, population will outstrip resources and lead to widespread dearth. Some modern scholars disagree with Malthus on the last stage of this process, however. While Malthus argued that the result would be famine, increased mortality, and a renewed cycle, historians now argue that many societies struggled along for centuries in such circumstances without renewing the cycle (an issue we will return to in future chapters). Regardless of who is right, poverty clearly increases according to both scenarios. As for the rise of commercial agriculture, this often arose in tandem with population growth and subsequent urbanization. Larger numbers of urban dwellers relied upon an ever-growing hinterland to supply their needs; this led to a greater focus on the part of landowners to grow for urban markets. Few landowners abandoned subsistence agriculture completely, but they allotted more and more arable land for planting crops that could be sold. Not surprisingly, as the profits from agriculture increased, so did the value of land, with patterns of land ownership shifting to emphasize consolidation. Sometimes, this gave rise to vast commercial estates like the Roman *latifundia*. The result was a spiraling increase in structural poverty among both rural landless laborers and urban workers whose salaries could not keep pace with the increasing price of food. Similarly, as commercial economies came to depend upon the size of agricultural yields and the profits to be made from them, the levels of conjunctural poverty flowed and ebbed with every harvest.

While many of the world's most advanced classical and post-classical civilizations witnessed these transformations, from ancient Rome and China to the Islamic Middle East, the most frequently cited example of such developments in the pre-modern world is medieval Europe. Up to the thirteenth century, Europe was a land-rich society growing prosperous in the wake of population growth, urbanization, and the rise of long-distance trade. Economic expansion and development were particularly evident in Italy and northwestern Europe, altering both the system of resource allocation and the nature of economic insecurity. In the countryside, the most significant changes included the spread of arable land, as an increasing population brought more land under cultivation, and the monetization of the economy. Seeking to acquire more goods from distant lands, many manorial lords converted dues in service and kind into money rents. This forced peasants to participate in market agriculture as a means of raising the necessary cash. In some areas, greater social differentiation resulted; some peasant families failed to prosper in this transition and survived by maintaining a small plot of land for their own needs and hiring themselves out to others who had acquired more land than they alone could work. In urban areas, change was even more dramatic. Although never more than 10 percent of the overall population of Europe, greater numbers of city-dwellers survived on the margins of the agricultural economy. Some participated in long-distance trade, manufacturing, transporting, and selling goods like woolen cloth and Eastern spices along an axis that stretched from southern England to the Middle East; others made and sold products to service the needs of urban residents. As in the countryside, economic development produced greater social differentiation. The urban social structure could range from escaped serfs, who often worked as day laborers, to a handful of nobles who preferred the more vibrant life of the cities to their country estates.

All of this had significant ramifications for Europeans' economic insecurity and susceptibility to poverty. But trade was brisk and the availability of land could meet the demands of population expansion through the end of the thirteenth century. During this period of economic growth, lords grew rich by collecting more rent from peasants who converted marginal lands into farms, while peasants sold high-priced grain to an expanding urban populace. In those urban areas, the woolen cloth industry in particular gave rise to the first signs of a mass market, employing thousands as fullers, spinners, and weavers in cities throughout Flanders and northern Italy. New urban wealth also sparked a building boom, marking this as the age of the great gothic cathedrals. In these conditions, poverty dogged mainly the elderly, orphans, and those who suffered an illness or handicap that ended their ability to take care of themselves or their families. Financial setbacks certainly afflicted many, but these often proved temporary during this period of economic opportunity.

This began to change around 1300, when population growth started to outstrip land. Heirs subdivided property into smaller and smaller plots, while depleted soil rendered meager harvests. Of course, the impacts of this progression struck various groups differently. In rural areas, those with the smallest plots of land suffered first and most severely. If the harvest failures were limited, those with larger holdings might actually profit. Food scarcity among a rising population meant higher prices for those with food, from middling farmers to great landlords. At the same time, as the number of rural workers increased, wages for those who sold their labor decreased, making it more difficult for them to meet their financial obligations. The same dynamic functioned in urban areas, where day laborers also faced more competition for jobs and lower wages. For such urban workers, however, harvest failures were even more damaging. Unlike their rural counterparts, most of these workers could not even count on the paltry yield of small household gardens. Higher prices for both food and lodging could easily send them into the downward spiral of poverty. Moreover, this had a rippling effect in the urban economy. As the costs for essentials increased, so the budget for additional manufactured products declined. For a time, the higher incomes of more fortunate rural landholders could make up the difference, but that market was easily saturated. Eventually, urban manufacturers, too, faced impoverishment. These were the markers of an organic economy in the throes of the transition from land-rich to land-scarce.

What makes fourteenth-century Europe notable was the drastic nature of the ensuing crisis, which included not just economic decline, but also social unrest and a massive death toll. The descent into poverty that began with overpopulation and commercial decline ended with crisis, thanks to a series of calamities that was to strike Western Europe. Problems began early in the century when agricultural yields started to fall. The climate exacerbated this, with a series of severe winters after 1315 leading to widespread famine between 1315 and 1317. Plague then struck between 1347 and 1350. This helped to precipitate an economic crisis, which the Hundred Years War between England and France (1337–1453) only exacerbated. The warring parties not only disrupted trade, but they also contributed to general impoverishment by raising taxes. In the cities, food prices skyrocketed as trade diminished. The wool trade, for example, ground to a virtual halt as the market collapsed, leading to unrest among the newly unemployed. In Florence, in 1378, for example, wool carders, known as *ciompi*, rose up against the wealthy merchants who dominated the city, but their revolt disintegrated as their new leaders proved unable to revive the city's economic fortunes and hold back the conservative forces marshaled against them. Unrest was no less common in the countryside, where, ironically, wealthy nobles began to feel the sting of higher prices; inflation and population decline convinced many lords to crack down on peasant tenants who sought to renegotiate the terms of their rents. In some areas, lords even revived manorial obligations, while those in the English Parliament passed the 1351 Statute of Labourers which attempted to decrease peasant mobility and hold down wages. By far, however, the clearest sign of increased poverty was the death toll itself. By some estimates, Europe lost approximately half of its population by 1350. While the bubonic plague accounts for the lion's share of this decline, which thus cannot be directly attributed to poverty, some historians argue that susceptibility to disease was heightened in Europe due to widespread malnutrition.

By the end of the century, as the crisis receded, Europe's socioeconomic landscape had been dramatically reshaped. Together, disease and warfare disrupted trade and altered consumption patterns. Europe's economy constricted and wealth was now concentrated in fewer hands. The vast woolen market dried up, the fledgling banking industry in Italy and Flanders limited its operations, and large expanses of newly cleared land reverted once again to fallow. The plague had depleted urban populations, but those who were left benefited from higher wages and low food costs. At the same time, manufacturing jobs were not as common as they had been and commerce had lost much of its dynamism. Luxury items now dominated trade. Although merchants made fewer trips East as the rise of the Ottoman Turks made such voyages dangerous, few diverted capital to other ventures. For their part, banks turned almost exclusively to government bonds. Overall, the mood favored short-term gains and immediate consumption, not long-term investments. In the countryside, the decreased population also translated into better conditions for many peasants. Despite their attempts to keep rents high and wages low, lords had to temper their interests or see their fields remain bare. However, low population levels meant that grain prices had also fallen. As in the urban economies, the vitality of the twelfth and thirteenth centuries had been replaced by stagnation. Ironically, lesser nobles often found themselves at the greatest disadvantage in this new economy. Their rents and agricultural goods no longer earned vast sums, but the luxury items necessary as markers of their social rank continued to command high prices. For Europe as a whole, prosperity would return only in the second half of the fifteenth century, crowned by the rise of a vastly expanded and significantly transformed world economy driven by Europe's conquest of the new world.

Europe's fourteenth-century crisis thus demonstrates many of the most prominent causes of poverty in the pre-modern world, from famine to warfare. At the same time, it illustrates how population growth and particular systems of resource allocation can leave some far more susceptible to those causes than others, while underscoring the myriad factors that can shape and shift the line separating the two. When Europe was best described as a land-rich society during the eleventh and twelfth centuries, long-term poverty and the possibility of starvation without assistance afflicted principally those who were physically unable to care for themselves. Poverty generally took the forms of individual destitution or large-scale conjunctural poverty. As the population began to outstrip available resources by the end of the thirteenth century, however, structural poverty and more limited forms of conjunctural poverty gradually emerged. Among peasants, the former struck those with insufficient land and decreasing opportunities to supplement that with paid labor, especially as population growth suppressed wages. For some, this hardship arose from the structure of the economy, when monetization prompted limited market agriculture and the gradual accumulation of land into fewer hands. For others, it was the result of over-population, as partible inheritance made it difficult to assemble enough land to meet subsistence needs. Conjunctural poverty, on the other hand, accompanied harvest failures, often made more harmful by rising taxes and rents. Among urban residents, poverty also accompanied harvest failures and over-population, but disruptions in trade aggravated this, making it difficult for day laborers to find employment that would pay subsistence wages. Eventually, with the arrival of the plague and large-scale warfare, crisis poverty emerged in the fourteenth century. When that crisis abated, poverty once again became an affliction that befell those who had lost the individual means to support themselves and their families, the destitute. It is worth noting, however, a new form of poverty slowly developing in this context among the lesser nobility. For the most part, they did not fear hunger. Rather, they cringed at the prospect of falling from their high status because they could not afford to live as standards dictated. As we'll see in future chapters, this type of poverty, although quite rare at this point in time, became more common in modern Europe.

Perceptions of poverty and charity

While it is thus possible to distinguish similar dynamics in the causes of poverty across cultural boundaries, discerning commonalities in perceptions of poverty and charity is much more difficult. Of course, popular perceptions are always difficult to gauge; this is particularly true of the pre-modern period, when few individuals left records of what they believed or how they regarded certain issues. It is unlikely, however, that any but those who lived in destitution, those who were in immediate need of food, clothing, and shelter, saw themselves as poor. In rural areas, most people lived very similar lifestyles, making and growing much of what they needed in an age that predated mass production and consumption. In cities, disparities of wealth and prestige were certainly starker and may have given rise to more nuanced definitions of poverty and a greater sense of self-identification among society's have-nots, but the urban population remained a small percentage of the whole. In addition, because the norms of most societies expected families to care for their own needy, only those lacking familial support were typically recognized as impoverished. Finally, with the potential misery of illness and harvest failure constantly in the background, everyone understood that no one was immune from hunger and want. Economic security was indeed a luxury that very few enjoyed. Perhaps because such hardship seemed to strike so haphazardly, attitudes toward poverty and charity are best found in the philosophical and metaphysical systems that civilizations devised to make sense of their lives. That means searching for such views in the world's major religions: Buddhism, Christianity, Hinduism, Islam, and Judaism. While most of these faiths placed far more emphasis on charity than poverty, it is difficult to address the former without discussing the latter.

For the most part, these religions defined poverty and wealth in material terms, or at least they recognized a material dimension to these conditions. As it developed in early medieval Europe, however, Christianity also characterized poverty in its relationship to power and prestige. Only after the commercial revolution of the twelfth century did poverty come to mean the absence of money, not authority and influence. While each religion thus conceptualized poverty similarly, there was much less consensus surrounding the value of poverty. Most of the world's religions saw little intrinsic worth in either wealth or impoverishment. In Buddhism, the emphasis falls on balance and voluntary simplicity. People with either too little or too much can easily become attached to the illusions of this world, and anxiety over the acquisition or loss of material possessions can distract from calm meditation. Hinduism, on the other hand, relegates poverty and wealth to stages of life. As householders, the second in the four stages of Hindu manhood, men should devote themselves to *artha*, or the acquisition of wealth, for their families are dependent upon their economic success. The first and final stages, however, are marked by poverty. A young pupil is expected to learn humility by begging for both himself and his guru, while an elderly man approaches death by renouncing all of his concerns in this world. As for women, their fortunes are attached to the life stages of their husbands; their lives progress from childhood to marriage. The connection between renunciation and spiritual rebirth gave rise to a vibrant tradition of asceticism in India, but all in all, references to poverty in the Hindu scriptures are rare. Even the material implications of the caste system received scant attention. It is interesting to note, however, that hunger was never related to karma; it is not the result of bad actions in a previous life. For its part, Judaism ascribed spiritual value to neither poverty nor wealth. Jewish teachings acknowledged inequality, but, as we'll see later, religious law expected observant Jews to minimize its impacts in the interest of economic justice. Overall, as with the other faiths, more attention is lavished on the subject of charity than poverty.

Only in Christianity and Islam did scholars focus significant energy on debating the merits of poverty. To a certain extent, both the Bible and the Qur'an lend themselves to such speculation. According to Luke, Jesus taught that "It is easier for a camel to pass through the eye of a needle than for a rich man to enter the kingdom of God," while Mohammad, in one of his visions, reported seeing more rich in Hell and more poor in Heaven. Early Christianity also developed a tradition of asceticism, which gave rise to monasticism in both the eastern and western branches of the religion. All of this led some medieval Christian and Islamic scholars to argue that poverty was inherently holy, more so if it was entered into voluntarily. According to Abu Hamid Muhammad al-Ghazzali, an eleventh-century Sufi mystic and scholar, poverty denoted a removal from the material concerns of this world and a complete devotion to God. Similarly, among some twelfth-century Christians, the community of Jesus' first believers, who held property in common and lived lives of material simplicity, represented the true religious ideal. Yet neither of these viewpoints represented the majority or, in the Christian faith, the institutional approach to poverty. Most Islamic scholars argued that both the rich and the poor faced challenges that tested their faith; the poor, for example, were often diverted from pursuing the knowledge of God in order to beg for their needs. Moreover, voluntary poverty was a symbol of personal will, and as such failed to recognize that only God's will mattered. Islam, according to this view, could not support a belief in voluntary poverty. Christianity, on the other hand, did acknowledge the merits of such hardship. But according to church doctrine, poverty was always just an instrument, not an end in itself. For the wealthy that divested themselves of their worldly possessions, such acts of sacrifice, and not the state of poverty itself, signified virtue. For those who already lived with need and want, acceptance of their lot with humility was the relevant factor. In this manner, according to historians, church officials were able to tame a new lay spiritual movement that arose in urban areas during the economic transformation of the twelfth century. The spirituality that initially spawned a new interest in the economic organization of the first Christian community was channeled into the creation of new mendicant monastic orders, like the Franciscans and Dominicans, which could be controlled by Rome.

If poverty provoked divided responses among the world's major religions, they all agreed that charity was a virtue. The principal differences arose from the place of alms and compassion within their dogmas; some placed more emphasis on the intent of the giver, while others devoted considerable energy to ensure that only the "deserving" benefited from generosity. For both Hindus and Buddhists, aid to the poor brought merit, but only if it was given without concern for that merit. Buddhism also supported a monastic tradition; the monks and nuns of the *sangha* were both the recipients of donations and a source of assistance to the lay poor. Care for family and friends, charity, and support of the *sangha* were the correct uses of wealth according to Buddhist teachings, which also made poor relief the provenance of both religious personnel and virtuous secular rulers. Judaism placed a different connotation on charity. The Hebrew word for charity, *Tzedaka*, also means justice. This implies that aid to the poor is not so much about generosity, as it is about redistribution and rectifying the relationship between the rich and the poor. The twelfth-century scholar Maimonides, the first to codify Jewish laws on charity, wrote not only that charity was best given anonymously, but also that the highest form of charity was to take a poor man into partnership, thus preserving his dignity and self-respect. In fact, in order to prevent extremes of wealth and poverty, the book of Leviticus dictated an ambitious land redistribution to take place during the Jubilee year. While many scholars doubt that this ever occurred in ancient Israel, it makes an important statement about Jewish values and ideals, especially the perceived need to alleviate the tensions caused by material inequalities. The prophetic literature, which dates from the ninth and eighth centuries BCE, also emphasized social and economic justice via such mechanisms as tithing and gleaning laws, debt release, and the emancipation of debt slaves. This concern with community relations is particularly evident in the Jewish ritual law, *halakha*, which states that "the poor of your household have priority over the poor of your city, and the poor of your city have priority over the poor of another city." In medieval Jewish communities this had the extra benefit of guaranteeing that those who received assistance were truly deserving of such generosity.

For its part, Christianity borrowed heavily from Jewish practices. Raised a Jew, Jesus took assistance for the poor as a given, a natural aspect of proper social relations. Yet charity lost its redistributive element as Christian doctrine developed. Instead, charity was to be practiced for the redemption of sin. Indeed, according to many early Christian scholars, poverty exists so that the rich may find salvation through almsgiving, which was institutionalized in the practice of tithing. At the same time, others argued that charity had to be voluntary. It was also best if it was rational, taking into account the consequences for both the recipient and the benefactor. By the end of the medieval period, this translated into a concern with assisting only the "deserving" poor. Typically, this reflected a growing fear of professional beggars, but it also excluded many of the able-bodied structural and conjunctural poor, unless their need arose from widespread calamity. Christian moralists also began to emphasize the plight of the "shame-faced" poor, those whose misery was especially difficult because they had once enjoyed a life of relative security and high status. Their honor prevented them from seeking assistance from public charitable institutions. As a result, charity took two forms: on the one hand, as with Buddhists, it was institutionalized in religious establishments, especially monasteries; on the other, private, individual gifts often went to support people whom the benefactors knew as members of their own social milieu. Regardless of the form, a notion of reciprocity characterized all charitable gifts. Popular perceptions expected recipients to assist their patrons, known or anonymous, by offering prayers for their salvation.

Of all of the world's religions, Islam is perhaps the most concerned with the subject of charity, for alms-giving is one of the faith's five pillars, or central tenets and obligations. All faithful Muslims must pay *zakat*, an annual alms tax, while Islamic scriptures encourage voluntary giving, or *sadaqa*, as a means of bringing the donor closer to God. For Sufi mystics in particular, assistance to the poor was more than just an obligation of the faith; it was also a means of demonstrating that one's love of God surpassed the love of property, and that one was thankful for one's blessings. Historians also argue that charity served several important secular functions in Islamic society. According to some, it purified and protected property. The rich could enjoy their luxuries with clear consciences and relatively free hands once they paid *zakat*, the amount of which varied depending upon the type of property being taxed. Others argue that charity served as a basis for the Arab economy during the first centuries of Islamic expansion. Wealth entered the economy as spoils of war, but since the poor had a right to assistance, such riches were not concentrated into a few hands. It circulated, for it was possible for a recipient of assistance to gather so much that they, too, became responsible for paying *zakat*. In this way, Islam encapsulated both the Jewish tradition of redistribution, which also harkened back to a pre-Islamic Arab gift economy, and the Christian emphasis on charity's spiritual benefits for the donor as well as the recipient. Islamic scholars also shared the Christians' concern that aid go to those who truly deserved it. Scripture dictated eight categories of beneficiaries, which included Muslims who could not provide for themselves or their families, indentured slaves, debtors, holy warriors who were not compensated by the state, needy travelers, and non-Muslims who supported Islam. Ironically, those whom the government charged with collecting *zakat* were also eligible to receive it. Of course, there was some disagreement over who on this list was most deserving, and what exactly constituted need. Al-Ghazzali, for example, argued that ascetics were most deserving, because they had abandoned the comforts of the material world. Next came those who were truly devoted to monotheism, for they recognized that God was the true source of their relief, while the giver was merely an instrument. They were followed by those who concealed their need; those who could no longer afford to live as they once had; those responsible for children or who were themselves ill; and, finally, relatives. It is important to note that relatives did not include the immediate family, for both family members and slaves had a right to maintenance, and thus could not become recipients of *zakat* unless the family breadwinner was incapable of performing his proper function. As for what constituted need, here, too, Islam came to mirror the Christian concern with the "shame-faced" poor. While a minority of scholars defined poverty in precise financial terms, the majority gradually adopted a status-based definition, since this was what determined maintenance. In other words, a laborer could expect less charity than a merchant, since his socioeconomic status required fewer material goods. Similarly, it was deemed proper to give *zakat* to a debtor even though he did not suffer from immediate need. Such disagreements over the appropriate forms and objects of charity only underscore its importance in Islamic doctrine.

Although Islam may have bestowed more attention on poverty and charity than the world's other great religions, one thing should be clear from this brief overview. Because need and want were prominent aspects of everyday life for all of humanity, anyone who sought to make sense of life had to address them. While it is impossible to know how their insights affected people's actions, they serve as an essential starting point for understanding the range of options that the world's civilizations devised for both preventing and alleviating poverty.

Strategies for avoiding and alleviating poverty

The institutions and traditions that the world's pre-modern civilizations developed to address and prevent deprivation separate into four broad categories: state-run establishments and practices, private institutions, family-based arrangements, and informal strategies. For both invalids and able-bodied individuals already suffering from need, the most common response, begging, falls into the final category. This was most effective in urban areas and during religious holidays. Hindu and Buddhist societies readily accepted begging since it was valued as a means of earning merit for benefactors. For Hindus, asking for alms also taught humility. In the Islamic Middle East, too, the spiritual benefits of informal charity encouraged begging, particularly in areas without functioning institutions of poor relief. Fear that beggars were "professionalizing" and that charlatans were taking advantage of the public's generosity, however, sometimes sparked hostility and distrust of the poor who sought assistance so openly, especially when beggars congregated with one another. Beggars also suffered from growing concern for the "shame-faced" poor. In the writings of al-Ghazzali, one of the most important Islamic scholars on the topics of poverty and charity, begging was condemned as a sign of open complaint against God. Moreover, it required the supplicant to humble himself before someone other than God, while negating the spiritual merit of charity by forcing the benefactor's hand. A similar dynamic developed in medieval Europe. In a few cities, officials went so far as to criminalize vagrancy, especially among the able-bodied. This placed many of the poor into very difficult straits and contradicted long-held traditions concerning aid to strangers. Both Christian and Islamic teachings, based partly on Hellenic and Jewish traditions, singled out needy travelers as deserving of charity, for they could not benefit from the solicitude of their families. Fortunately, unease with begging typically arose in environments where more formal institutions were available to aid the poor.

In most civilizations, the line separating these public and private charitable establishments was difficult to discern. Religious institutions frequently enjoyed official sanction and benefited from tax funds, while royal largesse often mixed those same taxes with the personal fortunes of the ruling family. Regardless of their provenance, however, most charitable institutions served similar functions. Chief among these was to assist the destitute, those who could not support themselves. Buddhist and Christian monasteries operated orphanages, for example, while Christian monks and nuns also staffed hospitals in some of Western Europe's major cities, many of which were built during the twelfth-century commercial revolution. These hospitals principally served the elderly and invalids without family to care for them, not those recuperating from illness. Monasteries also offered assistance to religious pilgrims, fulfilling the tradition of aid to wayfarers and strangers who had no family to support them. In Islamic lands, charitable endowments, or *waqf*, usually offered these same services. The *waqf* designated the profits from agricultural land or commercial real estate for a charitable project, like funding a hospital, orphanage, or even food distribution. In some instances, a founder might designate his own descendants as the chief beneficiaries of the *waqf*, but any surplus would also serve the community's poor. A *waqf* had political and economic benefits for its founder, too. In addition to being tax-exempt, a benefactor could use a *waqf* to establish bonds of patronage, while some women established them to protect their property from unwanted encroachment.

Beyond aid to the destitute, some states and institutions adopted programs that alleviated and prevented hardship for even able-bodied individuals. Food distribution, for example, was a mainstay for societies as diverse as the Roman empire, medieval Europe, and ancient China. In fact, beggars in medieval Europe often traveled from monastery to monastery according to a set calendar of distributions. Indeed, up until the twelfth century, monasteries were virtually the sole formal setting for assistance in Western Europe. The church designated between a quarter and a third of its revenue for poor relief, while benefactors frequently named monastic orders as the administrators of their charitable gifts and bequests. In China, Buddhist monasteries were also significant sites of aid for the needy, but unlike Europe, this in no way eclipsed the important role of the state, especially its attempts to manipulate the economy. In fact, a program of community granaries, devised by the neo-Confucian scholar and bureaucrat Zhu Xi in the twelfth century, was in part an effort to diminish Buddhism's appeal among the Chinese populace. But it also had roots in both traditional Confucian thought and an older imperial institution, the Ever-Normal Granaries. These granaries kept the price of rice stable, by buying it when the crop flooded the market and drove the price down, and selling it in times of scarcity to keep the price from soaring. According to Zhu Xi, the community granaries were more efficient because they avoided the bureaucratic entanglement that often accompanied control of the Ever-Normal Granaries. The imperial government also oversaw charitable granaries for direct assistance to the needy in a program established in the 1040s. Local officials kept registers of those eligible for rice allotments, like orphans, widows, and invalids, but the relief system could be expanded during harvest failures to include the able-bodied. Finally, under the Song dynasty reformer Wang Anshih, the state undertook an ambitious farm loan program, the "green shoots" scheme, which offered peasants loans during the planting season, which were to be repaid during the harvest. That the state would take such an activist stance is perhaps predictable given the economic vitality and volatility of the Song period and China's more secular, state-centered cultural traditions. No state in Western Europe could rival the church's reach, making it the more logical body to develop poor relief institutions, while Middle Eastern jurists prevented similar government-run operations by enshrining firm property rights in Islamic law, making it difficult to collect taxes in support of innovative agencies and programs.

Neither begging nor institutional assistance were attractive options for most individuals, however, for these strategies usually separated them from their homes and communities. Typically, only those without option turned to the outside for help. For the vast majority, then, security rested within the family or the community. In India and China, for example, the extended family maintained ancestral or lineage lands in order to support needy kin. During the Song dynasty, some Chinese officials even established granaries and schools for their descent group. According to one scholar, this may have reflected both the precariousness of life in a time of great social and economic change, and the changing nature of the state, with government positions and a family's survival coming to depend more firmly on successful examinations. Like the Muslim *waqf*, these charitable estates could offer a wide range of services, from monthly allotments of rice to funeral and marriage expenses. The majority of them, though, stipulated more vaguely that estate revenues should go to support members of the descent group. In this manner, charitable estates assisted those in need, while enhancing the leadership claims of the lineage's more successful branches, particularly since a single lineage could encompass an entire village. The immediate family, too, could become the site of harsh strategies for preventing a slide into poverty. Family limitation, for example, was a common response to impending dearth. Unfortunately, this often took the form of infanticide, especially female infanticide, for many cultures saw girls only as expenses. Older children might be sold into slavery, or in Western Europe, given to monasteries as oblates to be raised in the church. Decreasing fertility was another means of preventing poverty, but only in Western Europe did it become a widespread popular response. Although historians dispute the origins of the European Marriage Pattern, which decreased fertility by encouraging women to forestall marriage until their mid-twenties, there is ample evidence that during the Middle Ages, and particularly as land became scarce in the thirteenth century, many Europeans followed this pattern as a means of avoiding future hardships.[2]

Beyond the family, the community itself presented a number of strategies for enhancing security. Land distribution among village peasants was one such approach on European feudal estates. Every year, village elites would gather to divide up the strips of land that comprised their share of the lord's arable land. They usually apportioned it in a manner that ensured subsistence for everyone in the village; larger families received bigger shares, while everyone had a portion in the most and least fertile sections of the estate. In China, community granaries, where established, could also help village residents regardless of lineage. Perhaps the best known form of community self-help, however, was a product of urban society: the guild. In places as diverse as China, India and Europe, guilds performed many functions, but the most important of these decreased the insecurity of making one's living from commerce. Besides providing relief for members who had fallen on hard times, including funds to cover the expenses of illness and funerals, guilds limited competition and implemented policies that allowed all members to find their place in the market. According to this logic, the profit motive should give way to the just price, a price that would not undersell others in the craft. Some European guilds even stipulated that any member who benefited from an exceptional deal on supplies had to offer a share of those goods to his competitors at the same price. Regulations governing quality and wages had a similar goal and impact. Of course, these rules could also harm anyone who was not a master in the guild. Journeymen, for example, frequently complained that their needs garnered little concern among the leaders of the guilds. Women, too, usually the widows of masters, fared poorly in male-dominated guilds, sometimes being forced to remarry within the guild if they hoped to keep their shop. Limiting access for journeymen and women was thus another way that masters protected their economic interests, especially when markets constricted. Despite this, for journeymen and craftswomen, like peasants in the field, the community was an important source of security in the pre-modern world. Members were loath to abandon it in search of other forms of assistance, whether it came from the state, religious institutions, or even kind strangers passing in the street.

Conclusion

Many different factors shaped the lives of the poor, from systems of resource allocation to the range of formal relief institutions. It would be a mistake, however, to see those in need merely as the pawns of the rich and powerful. Options and strategies for survival arose from complex, tacit negotiation. Since the elite typically saw relief as a means of maintaining social control, the poor could always register their dissatisfaction through riot and rebellion or crimes like theft and prostitution. At the same time, most civilizations were confined by the limits of agricultural production. Formal relief was rare for those who had not yet descended into extreme want, often associated with migration and voluntary separation from native communities. Even then, concern that assistance go only to those deemed "deserving" was a common feature throughout the world. Frequently, this restricted aid to the destitute; those physically unable to support themselves. The remaining, able-bodied poor fell back on begging or lawlessness. The vast majority of the pre-modern population, however, those who lived lives of simplicity and vulnerability, were loath to separate themselves from the informal networks of self-help founded on family and community relations. They resisted becoming what their own societies defined as "poor". Perceptions of need and want thus also played a powerful role in molding choices among both those who offered assistance and those who sought it. This generated tremendous variation in a period when most civilizations survived with only tenuous interconnections. What follows is an examination of the changes and continuities in both poverty and relief as those connections grew and intensified.

Further reading

On hunger: Lucile F. Newman (ed.) *Hunger in History* (Cambridge MA: Blackwell, 1990); and Lillian M. Li, "Introduction: Food, Famine, and the Chinese State," *Journal of Asian Studies* 41.4 (1982): 687–707. On world religions and poverty: Michael Bonner, Mine Ener and Amy Singer (eds) *Poverty and Charity in Middle Eastern Contexts* (Albany NY: SUNY Press, 2003); Peggy Morgan and Clive Lawton (eds) *Ethical Issues in Six Religious Traditions* (Edinburgh: Edinburgh University Press, 1996); Ched Myers, *The Biblical Vision of Sabbath Economics* (Washington DC: Tell the Word, Church of the Savior, 2001); and Adam Sabra, *Poverty and Charity in Medieval Islam* (New York: Cambridge University Press, 2000). On medieval Europe: Bronislaw Geremek, *Poverty: A History*, trans. Agnieszka Kolakowska (Cambridge MA: Blackwell, 1994); and Michel Mollat, *The Poor in the Middle Ages*, trans. Arthur Goldhammer (New Haven CT: Yale University Press, 1986). On China: Robert P. Hymes and Conrad Schrokauer (eds) *Ordering the World: Approaches to State and Society in Sung Dynasty China* (Berkeley CA: University of California Press, 1993).

Chapter 2

Poverty in the emerging global economy

In 1551, after exploring and trading along the coast of West Africa, Captain Thomas Wyndham returned to England with the first cargo of sugar to arrive in an English ship directly from its place of production. By the end of the seventeenth century, the traffic introduced by that single vessel employed over 400 British ships, with an average cargo of 150 tons of sugar. By then, however, most of that lucrative freight came from vast plantations in the New World. Africa supplied a different, though no less profitable cargo, slaves. Those ships, and the commerce they provisioned, comprised what historians have labeled the Atlantic System, just one part of the new world economy that developed after Europe's "discovery" of the Americas. The integration of these new lands and their resources into global trade set the stage for Europe's subsequent rise to the pinnacle of world power in the nineteenth century. Between 1450 and 1750, however, Europe was simply one of many players on the global stage. Indeed, without the accidental advantage that the introduction of Old World diseases gave them in Latin America, Europe's military weaknesses confined them to small coastal outposts in Africa and Asia. In sub-Saharan Africa, for example, European slave traders could not merely seize slaves for transport to the Americas; they had to offer African traders merchandise of real value for the slaves they acquired. In China, some imperial advisors, feeling confident that Europeans were no match for strong ground forces, counseled a rejection of contact with these Western barbarians. Japan did just that in 1639, forbidding Japanese merchants from leaving the islands and closing all but one of its ports to Western traders; a small, closely regulated community of Dutch merchants remained on the island of Dashima in Nagasaki harbor. Outside of the Americas, then, European empires were chiefly commercial networks based around trading fortresses, not structures of direct domination.

Although not yet as strong and integrated as it would become after 1750, this new global economy left few immune to its impacts, and this is particularly evident in the history of world poverty. That is not to say that the forms and causes of impoverishment evident in earlier periods disappeared. Poverty still meant hunger; illness and old age continued to trigger destitution;

and harvest failures and systems of resource allocation that favored the few over the many still bred structural and conjunctural poverty. However, during these centuries, the world economy kindled the spread of additional forms of poverty, especially slavery, and forged close bonds between new patterns of trade and many traditional causes of economic insecurity. Of course, every civilization experienced these changes differently. In some, the world economy's impact was muted; it merely contributed to older sources of impoverishment, like over-population and political instability. Elsewhere, it fostered whole new systems of production and entitlement, like capitalism and the plantation economy, which had dramatic impacts on both the number of those living in poverty and the factors that made others susceptible to such misery. In addition, no major civilization escaped the high inflation of the sixteenth century, which most historians attribute at least in part to both the influx of Latin American and Japanese silver on the world market and population expansion fueled by New World crops like corn, sweet potatoes, and manioc.

This network of global trade thus presents a good starting point for understanding world poverty as it developed after 1450. This chapter begins with a brief survey of the nature and operation of this commerce, followed by a more extensive overview of the resulting patterns in the history of poverty during these centuries. Throughout, our focus remains on both the forms of impoverishment that arose as commerce intensified and the deepening ties between that trade and the causes of need and vulnerability. Of particular interest here are the growing significance of race as a marker of hardship in the Americas and the development of new economic systems that increased insecurity in various parts of the globe. Unfortunately, our data continue to dictate an analysis comprised of broad brush strokes; the discussion must concentrate principally on changing systems of entitlement and susceptibility rather than exact levels of poverty. Taken as a whole, these general patterns all reflect the growing place of global influences in the plight of the world's poor, whether they understood that connection or not.

The world economy

The world economy that emerged during these years differed significantly from all of its predecessors. First, it encompassed far more of the globe than the networks that had arisen from Mongol control of Central Asia in the thirteenth and fourteenth centuries and Muslim predominance in the Indian Ocean before then. It brought New World crops and minerals into a trading system that included, but was not limited to, African slaves, Indian textiles, Chinese porcelains, East Indian spices, and Western firearms. Second, and more important, it had a greater impact on the societies that participated in it. Before the sixteenth century, trade networks touched relatively few people beyond those areas directly surrounding trade routes. Only a small minority made a living from that trade or enjoyed the goods that traveled over their land and sea routes. That began to change when Portuguese explorers first rounded the Cape of Good Hope in the fifteenth century in search of more profitable sources of Asian goods. With the integration of the Americas, more and more the world's people came not only to consume foreign goods, but also to produce for the world market. Participation in the world economy could thus occasion substantial impacts. Some scholars have linked it to population growth based on New World plants like manioc in sub-Saharan Africa, the sweet potato in China, and the potato in Europe. Others emphasize even more far-reaching consequences. Indeed, some historians argue that the world economy shaped significant aspects of the different societies that participated in global trade. The most famous of these scholars is Immanuel Wallerstein.

In the new "world system," according to Wallerstein, the sixteenth-century world separates into roughly four groups: core, semi-periphery, periphery, and external. In the first three categories, the social structure, economic organization, and political systems of the various states followed predictable patterns depending upon their position within the world economy. Core states benefited the most from global trade, and in the process developed institutions designed to make the most of such commerce, from centralized states with more extensive bureaucracies to large standing armies. In the process, spectacular wealth allowed the bourgeoisie to loosen social and economic structures from their traditional feudal moorings. The most obvious examples of core states include England and France. In the semi-peripheries, states like Spain and Portugal grew rich by controlling trade in Latin America and the Indian Ocean, but did not develop the internal manufacturing that would have allowed them to retain that wealth. Wallerstein characterizes their political and social structures as polarized between a central government and a strong landed elite. Finally, peripheries produced raw materials for commerce controlled by the core. For this reason, they lacked an effective central government or were controlled directly by the core. To enhance their profitability, production rested on coercive labor practices that allowed only a small elite to prosper. As for the last, external, category, these states' most significant characteristic was a strong central state that allowed them to maintain their own relatively closed economic systems and remain outside the network of world trade. China and Russia stand as models for this approach.

Since the 1990s, however, Dennis O. Flynn and Arturo Giráldez have argued that the key to world trade was China, not the West. Driven by a growing population and the Ming dynasty's inability to support a paper currency, China's economy required vast amounts of silver to flourish. In addition, as silver's scarcity and value increased, many Chinese, including the state, converted their debt receipts, including taxes, into silver payments, a process described as the "silverization" of the economy. To attract that precious metal from abroad, China became the world's chief purveyor of high-quality manufactured goods. The true nexus of the global economy was thus Manila, a Spanish colony founded in 1571, and home to thousands of Chinese merchants. In essence, silver fueled the new world economy, and China's requirements directed the silver market. New output from both American and Japanese mines fed this demand, with Europeans acting simply as middlemen. Far from being an external, it was China's demand for silver that fueled an economic boom incorporating virtually the entire globe between 1570 and 1630. To some, this enriched China, leaving its subsequent decline to be explained by eighteenth-century developments. For Flynn and Giráldez, however, the resources required to maintain China's silver-based economy eventually represented a drain of wealth, for it prevented funds from being diverted to economic development.

Though each interpretation places the driving force of the new world economy in a different civilization, the nature of world trade was the same. It consisted of shipping something plentiful and inexpensive in one locale to a region where it was both scarce and valuable. Economists refer to this as "arbitrage trade." Silver thus flowed to China because it was more highly valued there than anywhere else. Similarly, Latin American agriculture specialized in market crops like sugar and tobacco because they were highly prized in Western Europe. While nothing inherently ties this type of commerce to impoverishment, as it developed around the globe between 1450 and 1750, the world economy had enormous consequences for world poverty.

Poverty and the world economy

Not all of these consequences were immediately perceived as such, however. Hunger, for example, remained the defining feature of poverty throughout much of the world. Yet the new network of trade spread two other forms of impoverishment. The first of these was slavery, which became the dominant labor form in Latin America. Conquistadors and the settlers who followed them brought with them disease and enslavement, decimating the native population and reducing the survivors to conditions that only a minority survived. Peru lost almost half of its pre-conquest population between 1570 and 1620, while Mexico's population plummeted from approximately 25.3 million in 1519 to only 1 million less than a century later. Most of these people fell victim to smallpox and other European diseases, like measles. Others died in the harsh conditions that the Spanish and Portuguese imposed to make their new territories profitable. Initially, Spanish colonizers won generous land grants from the crown that ceded them entire villages. According to this *encomienda* system, natives owed labor, goods, and food to their new lords, but maintained some of their own community structures until disease eventually destroyed even that. In Peru, where epidemics spared more lives, the discovery of vast silver reserves led to a similar labor system called the *mita*. This was a distorted and more deadly form of the old Inca labor tax, the *mit'a*, which had actually been a means of pooling resources and preventing impoverishment among the elderly. The new Spanish system compelled one seventh of adult male Amerindians to work for six months annually in mines, textile factories, or farms. Their wages were so meager that those remaining in the villages were obliged to send food for those toiling for the Spanish. Moreover, as the population continued to fall, the Spanish decreased the intervals between service from once every seven years to as little as every other year. As a result, many simply left the villages and became permanent wage labor in the towns that grew up around mines. By emptying the villages, this process destroyed an important means of preventing impoverishment. Workers lost some of the networks that sustained them in times of need; it took time to rebuild similar networks in the tumult of their new urban environments. In the Caribbean and Brazil, the plantation system was more prevalent. Like the *encomienda* and *mita*, however, the plantation reduced first Amerindians and then African slaves to a state that fits virtually all definitions of poverty, from the absence of choice to absolute need. Work and living conditions were so harsh that the average survival period for slaves on plantations was seven years. The combination of hard work and poor nutrition ensured that fertility among slaves remained low; growth came from the purchase of new slaves, not from natural increase. During the sugar boom of 1650–1800, slavers transported approximately 7.5 million Africans to the Americas. These men, women, and children comprised a growing population of structural poor. Despite their abilities, plantation managers and a harsh environment threatened their very existence. The very structure of the plantation economy thus kept them impoverished.

With the spread of coercive labor systems throughout most of the Americas, race became a significant marker of poverty in these nascent societies. In both Latin America and in British colonies in North America, Amerindians and Africans were more likely than Europeans and creoles, the Spanish term for people of European descent born in the Americas, to suffer from deprivation. To be sure, race didn't automatically condemn one to destitution, at least in Latin America. In fact, free blacks in Latin America were an important segment of the population. Many of these freed blacks had purchased their own freedom, making the most of their limited connections with the open market. This was more likely for urban slaves who worked as artisans and market women. This public presence of both freed blacks and slaves in Latin America promoted a society in which race did not necessarily indicate standing. Racial mixing, or miscegenation, enhanced that situation, with the creation of vast numbers of mestizos, children of European and Amerindian descent, and mulattoes, those of European and African descent. Nonetheless, the economy and culture that the Spanish and

Portuguese implanted in Latin America unquestionably placed Amerindians, Africans, and mixed-descent groups at a distinct disadvantage. In British colonies, racial ideals created much harsher conditions for blacks and Amerindians. Racial mixing was rare, and most whites considered blacks fit only for slavery. Manumission was much less common than in Latin America. Europeans weren't the only people with such prejudices; as the fourteenth-century Arab historian Ibn Khaldun wrote even before the conquest of the Americas, "the only people who accept slavery are the Negroes, owing to their low degree of humanity and their proximity to the animal stage." By drastically increasing the scope of the slave trade, and constructing an economy that rested so heavily upon such servitude, however, Europeans helped establish a connection between race and indigence in the Americas that endures to this day.

Like slavery, the second form of impoverishment to develop in the wake of the world economy, relative poverty, existed before 1450, but global commerce permitted it to take root more firmly in the more affluent societies supported by trade profits, particularly Western Europe. Building on the concept of "shame-faced" poverty, which arose during the Middle Ages, relative poverty defined need and want in relation to material possessions. One could be poor despite having met the basic needs of survival. Originally, such hardship plagued those with elite social status; it reflected an inability to live as social rank dictated. But, as former luxuries became more commonplace, like tea, coffee, and sugar, even ordinary people came to associate penury with the inability to afford these and the other items that supported Europe's fledgling consumer market. In addition to increased levels of consumption, this take on poverty also reflected certain cultural and political developments. Humanism, for example, convinced some Europeans that poverty was not part of God's plan. Unfortunately, this often translated into a condemnation of the poor, for if need were not divine, then it must signal a serious character flaw, especially among the able-bodied poor. At the same time, the formation of nation-states gave rise to higher expectations among ordinary subjects. A reliable monarch and a more developed bureaucracy were now supposed to ensure a ready supply of food. In short, hunger was no longer an acceptable or natural condition, permitting Europeans to reconsider the nature of poverty. Of course, such reconsiderations were themselves a luxury. For the vast majority of the globe, impoverishment meant the fear of starvation, and here, too, the emerging world economy had significant ramifications.

The most important of these consequences concerns the connection between the causes of poverty and economic insecurity, on the one hand, and the transformation of traditional systems of resource allocation and entitlement, on the other. In one scenario, land and labor were expropriated in order to focus on cash crops for long-distance markets. Perhaps nowhere were need and want more closely associated with this type of resource extraction than in Latin America, which suffered the introduction of the European-operated plantation system. Besides wreaking havoc with traditional societies and fueling the introduction of slavery and its miseries, plantations established new cropping patterns. Europeans seized the best lands and organized agriculture to suit their needs and interests. This resulted in what scholars label entitlement shortages. Many in Latin America lacked a nutritious food supply because they lost both access to land and control over their own labor, not because the land would no longer provide sufficient agricultural yields. This occurred not only in regions marked by plantations, but also in areas where the Spanish demanded taxes in cocoa or wheat, leaving little time or terrain for subsistence crops.[1] A similar economic dynamic emerged in Eastern Europe. In a process known as the second serfdom, peasants throughout this fertile region were re-enserfed to noble landlords who used high rents and extensive labor dues to maximize profits on the grains they sold to Western Europe's burgeoning cities. Though their lot was certainly better than that of Latin America's slaves, many of these serfs were now increasingly vulnerable to conjunctural poverty. Over-population, harvest failure, and especially excess appropriation could easily threaten their survival.

Very different production systems emerged in civilizations that grew wealthy from global trade. These societies, particularly Western Europe and China, developed advanced organic economies. Though still predominantly agricultural, these economies became far more commercialized, with independent farmers specializing in cash crops and a larger portion of the population making its living in manufacturing. In China, for example, global demand for silk meant devoting more arable land to mulberry trees. Workers in these regions, especially Jiangnan, relied on rice shipped in from other provinces. In fertile regions along the lower Yangtze, the growth of larger commercial towns prompted cereal farmers to abandon traditional crops for textiles, luxury foods, and other specialty items. Moreover, as China's population expanded, thanks in large measure to the sweet potato, which could be grown on smaller and previously unused plots, a thriving cottage industry emerged. Chinese manufacturers even developed proto-factories to produce goods with European specifications, copying Western motifs onto porcelain and wallpaper. Unfortunately, that left many vulnerable to downturns in world trade, such as the one that occurred in the mid-seventeenth century, when China's silver market flagged and a "mini ice age" decreased yields by shortening the growing season. At these times, workers and peasants throughout China swelled the ranks of the conjunctural poor.

Some historians argue that these changes represent the "buds of capitalism" in China, but this remains an issue of enormous contention. There is much more agreement, however, that the world economy did indeed contribute to the rise of capitalism in Western Europe. In simple terms, capitalism is an economic system that rests on private property and free exchange. Participants use capital, in the form of money, land, or production material, to realize a profit. Decisions on how best to use those resources for a maximum of profit rest on market forces, like supply and demand. In a relatively competitive and unregulated market, these typically conspire to force production to its lowest possible costs. In short, then, the goal is to make money, not to cement or maintain certain extra-economic relationships. Labor, in particular, becomes yet another resource, a cost of production to be controlled and minimized. The underlying philosophy behind capitalism belongs to Adam Smith, who, in his 1776 work *The Wealth of Nations*, promoted the argument that all in society benefited when individuals followed their own economic self-interest, for this forced each person to specialize in the endeavor for which they were most suited, making them more productive. Moreover, this system would instill a greater drive to be innovative. But, for this system to work to its potential, according to Smith, it must be governed solely by the "invisible hand" of market forces. No state or organization should be allowed to regulate trade and production, for that only protects those who are less productive and who would be better served by failing and searching for some new endeavor. These beliefs form the core of nineteenth-century liberalism, or laissez-faire economics. In reality, very few nations have followed this path; some form of regulated capitalism has become the norm throughout Western Europe, and by extension, most of the world.

Capitalism represents a significant departure from the manorial, gift, and guild economies that predominated in Europe before the fifteenth century. To explain this transformation, scholars have drawn on many factors, including the world economy, which, depending on emphasis, either directly or indirectly fueled capitalist development. It increased monetary flow with American silver, stimulated a growing market with exotic goods from foreign lands, and permitted some Europeans to grow fabulously wealthy and adventurous with that capital.[2] At the same time, with its potential to restructure so much of what Europeans had previously taken for granted, it could and did have drastic impacts on poverty and vulnerability. In brief, capitalism and the new economic conditions supported by world trade forced more and more of the European population into what the historian Olwen Hufton labeled the "economy of makeshifts." This left them far more exposed to the traditional causes of impoverishment, like famine and accidents, and weakened the customary practices that had previously allowed some to avoid seeking assistance outside the community. In particular, increased susceptibility arose from an almost complete dependence on labor in the absence of capital and land. In other words, survival rested on finding paid employment, either in urban workshops, on the large farms operated by a growing class of better-off peasants, or as workers in an expanding cottage industry of textiles.

Like their Chinese counterparts, these peasants and workers could easily slide into either structural or conjunctural poverty when market conditions deteriorated. Structural poverty struck especially in areas with high population density, which stretched resources thin, while conjunctural poverty mainly afflicted those whose livelihood depended on the vicissitudes of the market, a growing segment of the population. In rural areas, for example, population pressures in many areas led to the subdivision of land until plots grew too small to support a family, even at subsistence levels. In the new capitalist environment, such families easily fell into debt and lost their land to the new rank of middling peasants, those with more land than they alone could work. Traditional community bonds no longer secured access to a share of arable or commons, and capitalist landlords, who hoped to convert their estates into expansive commercial farms or to rent larger parcels to fewer more successful tenants, had little incentive to promote economic independence among all of their former serfs. In England, for example, almost 40 percent of the rural population had lost their land by 1700. Villages grew increasingly polarized, with the majority of peasants surviving on small holdings, supplemented with labor on larger farms or rural industry, like spinning and weaving. In urban areas, increased population meant falling wages. Insecurity became a fundamental trait of life for journeymen and unskilled migrants alike. For women, however, the urban economy was even less welcoming. Under the pressure of angry journeymen, some guilds that had initially opened their doors to women in the aftermath of fourteenth- and fifteenth-century population decline, now redefined their shops as male preserves. Female-dominated trades were notoriously low-paying. For unskilled single women, domestic service offered an attractive but dangerous option. Along with complete reliance on employers, most servants enjoyed housing and a secure source of food. Other women, particularly widows with children, were far less safe. Besides low-paying odd jobs, many of these women relied on prostitution as an essential means of feeding their families. Like their rural counterparts, the vast majority of urban residents thus depended upon an economy of makeshifts comprised of many different, yet insecure, sources of income. The fact that employment, wages, and profits were increasingly tied to the functions of global trade only enhanced that vulnerability. Farmers and their hired laborers, for example, specialized in commercial crops grown for the cities that grew rich on long-distance trade, like Amsterdam and London. At the same time, workers in those cities depended on orders from those who profited from the cargos unloaded everyday. In the final analysis, then, the result of capitalism was a stark increase in insecurity for many European men, women, and children. In fact, some historians argue that increased poverty was a key ingredient for further capitalist development, for it increased the ranks of wage laborers.

Besides triggering the rise of such new and precarious arrangements of resource allocation and entitlement as the plantation system and capitalism, the world economy also made more individuals susceptible to its own harmful impacts, like inflation. According to many historians, price increases like those experienced during the sixteenth century in Western Europe, the Ottoman empire, and China resulted from the greater availability of specie without a subsequent growth in the supply of goods on the market. People with more money were willing to pay more for the items they desired, driving down the value of their currency. Population growth, itself the product of widespread use of New World crops, increased demand and only exacerbated this process. In these regions, high prices were particularly harmful to those who sold their labor to survive, a population that grew as indebtedness became more prevalent. In China, for example, the silver gained from trade with European merchants was an important ingredient of the inflation that indebted many and eventually led to the peasant revolts that helped topple the Ming dynasty in 1644. Similar conditions prevailed in Europe, where the prices of most goods doubled between 1560 and 1600, while grain prices quadrupled. In 1500, for example, a construction worker in the German city of Augsburg could afford up to 1.5 times as many goods as a family of five might need with his annual salary. A century later, a builder's annual salary would buy only half of that, reinforcing the family's reliance on the makeshift economy. Even in good years, approximately 75–80 percent of an urban family's income went to food. In the countryside, too, food purchases took up a significant portion of the landless laborer's resources. In this situation, gainful employment offered little security. Rising prices prevented many families from building any sort of provident fund for the frequent accidents of early modern life. In Lyons, France, for example, probate inventories from the sixteenth and seventeenth centuries indicate that few people had furnishings or goods worth more than the equivalent of six weeks labor for the average silkworker, a common profession in that city. This left little margin for misfortune, from accident and illness to economic downturn and harvest failure.

It would be a mistake, however, to relate all instances of poverty and increased vulnerability directly to the world economy. In some parts of the globe, the impacts of world trade were quite ambiguous. For sub-Saharan Africa, for instance, questions about the impact of global trade on levels of indigence form part of the larger scholarly debate over slavery's impact. According to some historians, the marked loss in population, especially among the most productive portion of the populace, hindered African development. Slave trading also promoted warfare among tribes competing for the profits, and destroyed native production with the influx of European manufactured goods and Indian textiles. Even if Europeans paid high prices in a slave trade controlled by Africans, this benefited only a small few. For many others, this commerce meant hardship while the continent as a whole, once the site of a lucrative gold trade, now began a devastating slide in relation to its neighbors. Other historians counter, however, that slavery's impact was less detrimental on the continent than previously believed. While population losses were devastating, the damage was regional. Most slaves came from the inland regions behind the West African coast and Angola. These areas suffered the most. At the same time, new American food plants, like manioc, may have offset some of these losses. These increased the nutritional basis of local populations and opened new marginal lands to cultivation. Also, the decline in population may have owed as much to traditional causes like drought and famine as to the slave trade. In fact, recent research indicates that the two factors may have converged in the region around Angola. Drought in the grasslands forced many to migrate, a process that led some into the hands of Angolan slavers. As for European goods, these scholars argue that this supply supplemented African manufacturing; it was never extensive enough to offer detrimental competition for native artisans. Unfortunately, because these goods were destined solely for consumption, neither did they present new opportunities for economic development. Finally, there is little evidence to prove that Africans became more warlike than they had been in the past or than other civilizations, like Western Europe. Instead, slavery became simply another aspect of the traditional wars that regional competition sparked. Overall, then, the new world economy offers fewer explanations of poverty in sub-Saharan Africa than elsewhere. On the one hand, the loss of approximately 8 million Africans to the Atlantic slave trade decimated some regions. Certain villages and families clearly suffered destitution after the loss of valuable breadwinners. On the other hand, many parts of the continent remained relatively untouched by the new trade. In these regions poverty remained the product of drought, accident, illness, and warfare.

Conclusion

Between 1450 and 1750 the outline of the modern world began to take shape. The global economy that arose from European exploration, and the subsequent integration of the Americas into an emerging world network of trade, began a significant reshuffling of the major civilizations. Western Europe's star clearly rose as China's and the Ottoman empire's began to wane, though many in Asia and the Middle East wouldn't acknowledge this until the late nineteenth century. At the same time, new societies took root in the Americas, built upon a dependent relationship with Europe that would only intensify after 1750. While some regions remained relatively isolated, like Japan, Russia, and sub-Saharan Africa, they would soon have to confront a vigorous Western Europe, made more powerful thanks to the wealth generated from world trade.

It is no accident that these same centuries also witnessed the evolution of a new countenance on the age-old problem of need and want. Where the poor once comprised mainly the destitute, those relative few who could not provide for their own subsistence, especially the orphaned, the aged, and the infirm, that designation now expanded to include more able-bodied adults who had lost a traditional source of security in skill or land tenancy. Structural and conjunctural poverty became both more widespread and more readily associated with the everyday functions of commerce, not crisis. As the world economy increased the population that survived from wage labor and the market, it left them vulnerable to the fluctuations inherent in global trade. Chinese peasants and European urban migrants feared poverty not just because of illness and famine, but also because price increases could easily consume the near totality of their incomes and force them into debilitating debt. At the same time, the social consequences of intensified exchange among civilizations also drew a stronger connection between indigence and certain markers like race and gender. In the Americas, the widespread enslavement of Africans and Native Americans doomed many to lives of hardship and want. Even those who escaped lives of servitude saw prejudice dramatically limit their opportunities for amelioration. For women, too, new commercial economies could prove detrimental in myriad ways. In Western Europe, for example, traditions of community policing that had earlier limited illegitimacy broke down by the eighteenth century as young men fled their responsibilities for new urban horizons and left their pregnant girlfriends to fend for themselves back home. At the same time, new commercial practices often left women at a distinct disadvantage. Defined primarily through the adult men in their lives, most single women were shut out of all but the lowest-paying occupations, while wives and mothers were often perceived of as helpmates, not skilled artisans in their own right.

These characteristics that we associate with poverty today sank their roots in the world economy of the sixteenth and seventeenth centuries. Of course, global forces could also help stave off hunger, as American crops trans-planted into traditionally infertile soil helped offset the ravages of slavery in parts of sub-Saharan Africa and sparked population growth throughout the rest of the world. More often than not, however, the new environment that emerged from enhanced contacts increased the insecurities of life for much of the world's population. In short, the principal sources of poverty differed little from earlier centuries; rather, change derived from the greater number of men, women, and children who found themselves vulnerable to a break-down of their new economy of makeshifts.

Further reading

On the world economy and its impacts: Immanuel Wallerstein, *The Modern World System*, 3 vols (New York: Academic Press, 1984–9); and Dennis O. Flynn and Arturo Giráldez, "Cycles of Silver: Global Economic Unity through the Mid-18th Century," *Journal of World History* 13.2 (2002): 391–427. On slavery and its impacts: Herbert S. Klein, *African Slavery in Latin*

America and the Caribbean (New York: Oxford University Press, 1986); and Patrick Manning, *Slavery and African Life* (New York: Cambridge University Press, 1990). On capitalism's development (or lack thereof): Robert S. DuPlesssis, *Transitions to Capitalism in Early Modern Europe* (New York: Cambridge University Press, 1997); and Timothy Brook, *The Confusions of Pleasure: Commerce and Culture in Ming China* (Berkeley CA: University of California Press, 1998).

Chapter 3

Innovations in early modern poor relief

In 1596, the merchant capitalists governing Amsterdam introduced a new tool in their battle against vagrancy, the *Rasphuis*. This was a workhouse to incarcerate and reform the men arrested for the new crime of begging in the city. In accordance with its dual goals, the *Rasphuis* came equipped with a room to punish inmates who refused to do their fair share of the work that helped fund the institution. Administrators placed recalcitrant men into this cell and then let it fill with water. Forced to use a hand pump to save themselves from drowning, these men learned in a very literal sense that only hard work would ensure their survival. For historians, the *Rasphuis* captures the significant transformations that occurred in European poor relief during the early modern period, from secularization to a new emphasis on the redemptive power of labor. These changes inevitably altered the range of options that Europe's poor had come to rely upon in their strategies to endure. Throughout the Middle Ages, individuals hoping to prevent a disastrous slide into poverty turned principally to their family, neighbors, or, in urban areas, occupational group. For those unfortunate enough to have lost that struggle, relief could come from those same sources, and from formal institutions operated by the church, begging, and, in desperate cases, crimes like theft and prostitution. Despite some variation, especially in the range of formal institutions open to the poor, these strategies were basically the same throughout the pre-modern world. And, between 1450 and 1750, they remained basically the same in much of the world. Thus, while the world economy slowly introduced a new dynamic in the history of poverty around the globe, only in Western Europe did this translate into dramatic alterations to the structure of poor relief.[1]

The reasons behind this curious state of affairs are varied. In much of the world, rulers either saw little cause to alter traditional systems of relief or lacked the funds to reform them. In China, for example, the emperors of the Ming and Qing dynasties (1368–1644 and 1644–1911 respectively) used state funds mainly to defend their control of insecure borders and to quell internal unrest. As state charitable institutions like the imperial granaries suffered from neglect, local gentry assumed responsibility for their upkeep, guaranteeing continuity in assistance programs. In the Ottoman empire, too, a general decline in imperial finances and the rise of regional factionalism stymied any chance of reform. The poor remained reliant chiefly on traditional strategies, like begging and various *waqf* (religious charitable endowments). Western Europe, on the other hand, underwent considerable socioeconomic and cultural change that directly triggered a growing interest in reorganizing poor relief. Capitalism not only increased economic insecurity, but it also weakened traditional communal bonds of mutual assistance. This was particularly harmful in the countryside, leading more peasants to choose migration to the city as the best means of survival. This intensified pressure on urban officials to revamp relief schemes both to cope with the rising number of petitioners and to send a message to potential migrants that assistance was limited. At the same time, the spread of humanism and the Reformation changed attitudes toward work, poverty, and charity. Even in Catholic areas, secular authorities assumed greater responsibility for ensuring employment and protecting society from feckless and deceitful beggars.

Because innovations in relief were thus limited chiefly to Western Europe during the early modern period, this chapter focuses only on that region, with special emphasis on changing attitudes toward poverty and charity on the one hand, and new rules and institutions designed to assist the poor on the other. Though a uniform direction can sometimes be difficult to discern, these changes reflect an increasing concern with poverty and a dedicated search for the best means of alleviating it in an age of capitalist development, cultural ferment, and state formation. Overall, Europe's elite chose a path that emphasized deterrence and discipline, one that limited the descriptor "deserving" to a relative few, while recognizing that economic conditions sometimes dictated more expansive programs than their rhetoric supported. Although these developments had little impact outside of Europe before 1750, as the West later asserted its dominance over the rest of the world they became valuable models when adapted to new contexts.

New attitudes toward poverty and charity

The most significant shift in early modern Europeans' outlook on poverty was the growing belief that indigence was a moral scourge. Except in Catholic areas, and only for those who voluntarily assumed it in the confines of religious enclosures, need and want lost their spiritual value and respectability. To many historians, this was the natural consequence of capitalism. As private property became the foundation for both economic success and full civic independence, European society came to associate personal value almost completely with material possessions. A logical corollary thus held that hardship and need, particularly among the able-bodied, must be the result of personal character flaws. Evolving Protestant values helped to cement this new connection between personal shortcomings and impoverishment. Many Protestants not only emphasized individual responsibility, but they also preached the merit of all occupations or "callings." In other words, according to these theologians, God rewarded those who devoted themselves wholeheartedly to the ethical practice of their worldly professions. Indeed, to some, like the Calvinists, business success was a sure sign of being among the "elect." In addition, by rejecting good works as a path to salvation, Protestants effectively destroyed the last tie between poverty and traditional Christian morality. The growing prominence of science in the seventeenth century did nothing to challenge this correlation between poverty and moral failings. Science placed emphasis on humankind's control over its environment. Accordingly, poverty became less "natural." It was the result of human actions, not divine providence. Though less firmly rooted in Christian doctrine, impoverishment thus retained a moral dimension as a reflection of sloth, imprudence, and profligacy. While destitution, the physical inability to meet the needs of basic survival, continued to merit care and kindness, it became increasingly difficult for those who suffered from structural and conjunctural poverty to fit into the category of "deserving" poor.

In many elite eyes, indigence among the able-bodied also represented a political and social threat. This was particularly true after the Reformation began to foster groups that espoused egalitarianism and redistribution. The first alarming sign that Protestantism might foment rebellion was a German peasant revolt in 1525, but the peasant demands were more traditional than progressive. Indeed, many historians argue that this revolt was principally a reaction against capitalist encroachment on customary economic practices. During the English Civil War of the seventeenth century, however, religion served as a basis for much more radical designs on the political and social structure. This was more sophisticated and widespread than the attitudes captured in the rhyme "When Adam delved, and Eve span / Who was then the gentleman?" which gained popularity during the 1381 English peasant rebellion. The best known of these new groups was the Levellers, who rejected social class as a basis for political representation. Though most Levellers stopped short of socioeconomic egalitarianism, some argued that true political liberty was inexorably tied to property. This attitude helped spawn a splinter group known as the Diggers, or True Levellers, who argued for land redistribution among the poor. As Gerard Winstanley, a leader of the Diggers, put it: "true religion and undefiled is to give everyone land freely to manure [cultivate] co-operatively." The Diggers even established a short-lived commune on unused common lands at St George's Hill in 1649, fully expecting to act as a model for all poor and dispossessed English farmers and to prompt a popular renunciation of private property. In addition to these egalitarian experiments, fear and distrust of the poor also arose from the disruption of traditional social networks in capitalism's wake, for increased mobility and economic competition made the poor more numerous, rootless, and noticeable, especially in cities that attracted those job-seekers who had been forced to abandon the land. The transition to wage labor in both rural and urban environments proved particularly hazardous for those who fared poorly in job markets, especially the elderly and women. Among the latter, many faced the difficulty of balancing family commitments with the economic bias of low wages and limited opportunities, a situation that often condemned them and their children to misery. Ironically, then, as socioeconomic and cultural change made many of the poor less deserving of assistance, it also made it more imperative for society's "haves" to address the needs of the "have-nots."

Evolving attitudes toward indigence thus naturally influenced ideas concerning charity. First, given their new prominence as a signifier of moral degeneracy and potential social disorder, structural and conjunctural poverty now demanded relief that would concentrate on reshaping the character of the poor and controlling their capacity for revolt. Many of the innovative practices and institutions discussed below thus reflect these newly perceived needs. Second, according to a number of scholars, Europe's elite also transformed poor relief to meet the needs of a budding capitalist economy. Institutions like the *Rasphuis*, for example, emphasized the value of toil and created a more disciplined and docile workforce, while public outdoor relief, or assistance distributed to those residing outside of specialized relief institutions like hospitals and workhouses, regulated the labor supply, ensuring that seasonal unemployment or periodic economic downturns did not end in mass migration from a region that might need workers in a few months time. In addition, certain industries depended upon the labor of workhouse inmates. In seventeenth-century England, the increased quantities of spun yarn produced in workhouses helped break a bottleneck in cloth manufacturing, a vital industry in the European economy. Finally, besides these economic benefits, Europe's wealthy expected poor relief to enhance the prestige and status of benefactors. Many recently enriched merchants, for example, pinned their hopes for social mobility on participation in, and the endowment of, new municipal charitable schemes and institutions. For secular authorities too, especially monarchs seeking to assert their influence, public assistance enhanced the role of the state and legitimized its personnel. Since urban areas acted as a nexus for all of these developments, such new approaches to poverty and relief were most evident in Europe's burgeoning cities. Note, however, that change had its limits; European elites entertained no thoughts of redistribution. In fact, they reserved compassion almost exclusively for the destitute and the shame-faced poor, members of their own class too proud to seek assistance openly. For all others, new relief institutions were meant to be painful and humiliating.

Institutional change in charity and relief

Despite significant variation, usually resulting from religious and socioeconomic conditions, it is possible to discern two broad directions in the transformation of European poor relief: rationalization and an increased emphasis on moral reform. Of these, the most obvious was the tendency toward rationalization. Typically, that process also entailed secularization, for the reorganization of relief frequently involved enhancing the role of secular forces and enlisting the help of the lay population. Of course, in Catholic areas the church fought this process vociferously, for it opposed any limitations of its traditional purview. As a result, the extent of such change often reflected the power of the church in various regions. Spain, for example, experienced less change than France. It would be a mistake, however, to link the reorganization of relief and the growing role of secular authorities too closely with Protestantism. Indeed, the four most common aspects of this process were common to both Catholic and Protestant areas. These consisted of (1) the prohibition of begging; (2) the attempt to find more secure sources of funding; (3) the desire to define and then restrict aid to the "deserving" poor; and (4) the creation of new institutions to oversee assistance. Historians normally date the start of these reforms from the 1520s, when officials in cities like Paris and Ypres promulgated new principles for the organization of municipal assistance. The development that has attracted the most attention from scholars, however, is the set of regulations known collectively as the Elizabethan Poor Laws.

In many respects, the relief system in sixteenth-century England was ripe for overhaul, for between 1536 and 1540 the crown undercut traditional charitable institutions by closing the monasteries and seizing their lands. At the same time, new capitalist agricultural patterns advanced quickly in England, spurred on by a process known as enclosure. In the past, villages had protected their residents by deciding together how the estate's arable land should be distributed and by enforcing open access to various "common" parts of the manor, like fields and forests. Enticed by the profits to be had through commercial agriculture, however, estate owners began to enforce direct control over all of their land, enclosing it and reducing many peasants to wage labor. Those who could not find work usually migrated to the cities, attracted by the opportunities afforded by the new commercial economy. As cities strained under the weight of this new mass of impoverished, both municipal and national officials recognized the need for change. English poor law thus gradually unfolded through a series of Parliamentary statutes passed between 1531 and 1601, which urban leaders supplemented with their own efforts to fund and establish new institutions. Of particular interest in these reforms was the system of poor rates, or taxes to fund poor relief. In 1536, Parliament first empowered local officials to position "common boxes" in churches to centralize the collection of donations, while openly discouraging casual, indiscriminate charity, not least by criminalizing begging. Many cities throughout Europe had already instituted this reform, but English policies crossed into new territory when they authorized towns to make such contributions mandatory in 1552. Historians estimate that as late as 1660, only one third of them did so, but "poor rates" became virtually universal by 1700. Although England stood alone in both the national scope of its poor relief and its mandatory nature, it shared underlying concerns about poverty with the rest of Western Europe. The establishment of common boxes or chests was widespread, while scholars believe that voluntary contributions on the continent kept pace with English poor rates.

English lawmakers also reflected general patterns in their efforts to define the population most deserving of assistance. According to Parliament, able-bodied beggars definitely did not belong in that category. Indeed, much of the legislation passed during these years concentrated more on means of repressing vagrancy than on ways to administer relief. In 1598 and 1601, however, Parliament did designate the poor rates for outdoor relief. In addition, by 1660, English law authorized local overseers to repatriate any person eligible for relief but living outside of their city of origin or legal residence. This made it imperative for local administrators to maintain accurate records. Some towns even began to take censuses of the poor and to post rosters at distribution centers, while others obliged overseers to visit recipients regularly to ensure eligibility. For the most part, registered paupers consisted of those traditionally defined as worthy, i.e. widows, orphans, and invalids. But, in 1576, Parliament urged administrators not to neglect "poor and needy persons willing to work." In essence, English poor relief began to move beyond assistance for the destitute and acknowledged the structural poor, a category that grew as capitalism developed. Full recognition of their need had to await the end of the eighteenth century, however, when English towns implemented what is known as the Speenhamland system, which specifically designated assistance to supplement wages and tied amounts to the price of bread and the size of recipient families. Not only did this expand relief rosters, but it also shifted the majority from widows and orphans to male heads of household.

Further recognition of the able-bodied poor came in the final aspect of the tendency toward rationalization, the rise of new institutions. Outside of England, where national governments were less prominent in the reorganization of relief, some of these establishments helped to centralize and administer urban assistance. The *Aumones-générales* in large French cities like Paris and Lyon, for example, and the *bureaux de charité* in smaller French towns arose in the first half of the sixteenth century to coordinate and oversee municipal outdoor relief programs, many of which asserted lay control. In some instances, their assistance included raw material like linen, wool, and hemp that recipients fashioned into marketable products, with the profits reverting to the city. For those who had yet to suffer from impoverishment, especially potential victims of conjunctural poverty, new networks of public pawn banks, or *monti di pietà* as they were known in their original Italian, provided low-interest or interest-free loans. *Monti frumentari*, or grain banks, functioned as a rural counterpart, lending seed corn or food and expecting repayment only after harvest. Finally, by the eighteenth century, more and more cities and towns were turning to public works as a means of assistance. These schemes, like the French network of charity workshops, mainly served as palliatives for unemployment and indicate the growing place of assistance as wage subsidies or responses to periodic economic fluctuations.

The most prominent new institutions, however, comprise what Michel Foucault termed "the Great Confinement", the attempt to remove deviants, especially the idle poor, from the general population so that they might be disciplined and reformed. As such, they represent a crossroads of the two general directions of change in European poor relief, rationalization and moral reform. In some places, this entailed revamping the hospitals once reserved for invalids and pilgrims, though it also built on a tradition of isolating lepers in special houses. Paris' *hôpital général*, founded in 1656, is often cited as the perfect example of this development. This general hospital encompassed at least five separate institutions housing orphans, prostitutes, expectant mothers, and beggars of both sexes. But they all had one thing in common; each institution contained a workshop. Sometimes, the hospital operated the workshops on its own. At other times, administrators leased them out to area merchants or formed cooperatives. Unfortunately, they rarely earned a profit. Nonetheless, hospital officials considered the workshops valuable investments in the reform of society's impoverished. That was well worth the strain on their budgets. Work, discipline, and reform were even more intricately intertwined in the workhouse. The model for these establishments was Bridewell, founded in London in 1553. That the crown willingly surrendered Bridewell Palace, which had previously been used to house visiting foreign monarchs and dignitaries, is a testament to the growing concern with poverty and moral reform. This institution became so infamous that when the Parliamentary statute of 1576 demanded the construction of "houses of correction" in all English counties and towns, these became popularly known as "bridewells." And, as the example of Amsterdam's *Rasphuis* demonstrates, these soon spread from England to the continent. Together with more preventive forms of moral education, like schools for children from impoverished families, general hospitals and workhouses reveal the growing connection in European culture between poverty and moral failings.

Conclusion

To a certain extent, the transformation of poor relief in early modern Western Europe sent contradictory messages. In the sixteenth century, the elite launched a war on idleness that frequently translated into some form of incarceration for the able-bodied poor. Destitution warranted compassionate assistance, but structural and conjunctural poverty implied personal failure, particularly if it forced the victim into a life of begging. For many, the lazy beggar and the unwed mother of questionable morality dominated the new image of poverty. Each of these stock characters warranted discipline. In addition, elites increasingly recognized that poverty among the able-bodied could breed discontent and lead to dangerous social experimentation, while well organized poor relief promised economic benefits for those concerned with the availability of affordable labor. Regardless of cause, then, confinement and education seemed the appropriate keys to alleviating and preventing impoverishment. This focus on detention began to change by the eighteenth century, however, as a new approach slowly emerged in the shadows of the general hospital and workhouse. Outdoor relief and public works schemes, though never completely eclipsed by the strategy of confinement, appeared better able to address the needs of the working poor. Culminating in programs like the charity workshops, many poor relief administrators slowly acknowledged that structural and conjunctural poverty represented the new face of misery. For some, the "deserving" poor began to encompass those who had the ability to work, and who might even have a small parcel of land or paid employment, but who could not earn enough to support themselves or their families. Relief officials continued to insist upon assessing the moral character of those they helped and to believe that tackling need and want included shaping the behavior of assistance recipients, but they also came to accept that the new economy taking shape around them made charity an essential ingredient of the economy of makeshifts by which so many survived. While their power to influence poor relief was limited, some historians argue that the poor themselves may have been partly responsible for the declining interest in confinement by the eighteenth century. Since economic insecurity was a constant concern for many, popular attitudes grew increasingly hostile to workhouses even among those who managed to avoid its rigors. In fact, the fear of confinement possibly counteracted the community breakdown fostered by capitalism in some areas. Of course, their influence was insufficient to abolish completely the workhouses, which remained viable institutions well into the nineteenth century.

Within this ebb and flow in European poor relief during the early modern years, certain patterns deserve special attention. These include the prohibition of begging and the experimentation with confinement. The innovations with the greatest impact on future developments, however, were the enhanced role of the state, the rising concern with the working poor, and the new focus on moral reform and behavior modification. Once industrialization and imperialism began their transformation of the world economy, these alterations in traditional attitudes and approaches would have enduring impacts not just in Western Europe, but around the globe, too.

Further reading

On European poor relief: Bronislaw Geremek, *Poverty: A History*, trans. Agnieszka Kolakowska (Cambridge MA: Blackwell, 1994); Robert Jutte, *Poverty and Deviance in Early Modern Europe* (New York: Cambridge University Press, 1994); Catharina Lis and Hugo Soly, *Poverty and Capitalism in Pre-industrial Europe* (Hassocks: Humanities Press, 1979); and Paul Slack, *Poverty and Policy in Tudor and Stuart England* (New York: Addison-Wesley, 1988).

Chapter 4

Industrialization, imperialism, and world poverty, 1750–1945

In June, 1906, peasants in the Egyptian village of Dinshawai attacked a group of British soldiers who had inadvertently set fire to the village threshing grounds while hunting pigeons. Determined to use the incident as a warning after one of the soldiers died from his wounds, the British demanded that a special tribunal try and punish the perpetrators. In the end, officials hanged four villagers and imprisoned or publicly flogged sixteen others. This confrontation illustrates two fundamental features of world history between 1750 and 1945. First, it highlights the authority that industrialized powers enjoyed around the globe. Dinshawai inflamed passions precisely because it pitted an Egyptian court against Egyptian peasants all at the behest of Great Britain, for the British enjoyed de facto dominion over the country despite Egypt's nominal autonomy. Moreover, the hunting party that sparked the incident was either ignorant of or chose to disregard the fact that many peasants raised pigeons as food. In the eyes of Dinshawai's residents, British soldiers had set fire to their assets while hunting their property. The public execution of friends and neighbors demonstrated to all, however, that Europeans controlled both resources and lives wherever they went. That strength arose from industrial might, which, by the twentieth century, fueled similar imperialist claims by Japan and the United States. Second, the popular anger that eventually took so many lives denotes the pent-up rage that coursed below the surface in many colonial societies. This resentment sprang from the economic and social dislocations that accompanied imperialism, for industrialized nations typically used their power to restructure the world to suit their interests. This usually meant the destruction of traditional patterns of agriculture and manufacture in order to feed the industrialized nations' growing appetite for raw materials. Between 1750 and 1945, then, the world economy expanded and intensified, drawing the various parts of the globe together as never before. All of this had dramatic ramifications for the history of poverty.

Industrialization and imperialism fundamentally altered the outlines of world poverty by transforming the way wealth was generated around the globe. This introduced two significant alterations to the patterns and characteristics we have already seen. First, the defining characteristics of poverty changed. In particular, it became less life-threatening by the middle of the twentieth century. In Western Europe and Japan, industrialization broke the land constraint that had previously doomed societies to impoverishment when population began to outstrip the productive capacity of agriculture. It offered a seemingly endless source of wealth built on the manufacture and consumption of material goods regardless of population growth. Thus, although it was unevenly distributed, the world generated more wealth during these centuries. At the same time, new forms of transportation and more efficient states drastically reduced the mortality arising from famine and severe food shortage. Industrial capitalism also dictated the abolition of slavery, for wage labor had the added benefit of making workers consumers, too. Finally, as we will see in the following chapter, states began to take a more active interest in protecting the welfare of their citizens. In this new environment, poverty came to mean malnutrition and not chronic hunger in much of the world. Specialization in cash crops replaced subsistence agriculture; arable lands accumulated in fewer hands; and many people lost their connection to farming and increased their dependence on the market for foodstuffs, particularly for the basics of a healthy diet. Often, the poor were able to stave off undernourishment, but they did so by relying on cheap staple crops that supplied insufficient nutritional value. Meanwhile, in industrial societies, wealth and consumerism expanded the ranks of those who experienced need as relative poverty. This was especially true as these societies matured. Thus, by the dawn of the twentieth century, the number of malnourished declined in Western Europe, but this only increased the number of those judged poor because they could not afford to partake in "normal" consumption patterns. For a growing portion of the world's population, then, poverty became penury or pennilessness. They were no longer expected to produce the food and goods they needed, nor could they afford to purchase the requirements of a nutritious diet or the consumer products that marked social inclusion.

The growing importance of the market underscores the second major alteration in world poverty. Industrialization and imperialism left far more of the world's people vulnerable to need and want because they became dependent upon wage labor and market relations for their survival. This weakened their entitlement to both surpluses and the necessities of life. Farm workers who grew food for a wider market, for example, had a weaker claim to crops than distant consumers with higher incomes. Dependence on wage labor also altered the causes of structural and conjunctural poverty. Structural poverty, which afflicted those with the physical ability but not the means to subsist, previously struck those who lacked a direct connection to the means of production, often in the form of land, or who lost control over their own labor, like slaves. Now, it typified the plight of the unemployed and the thousands of men and women whose salaries proved inadequate to make ends meet. This was as true of industrial economies dominated by factories as it was of agricultural societies marked by commercial farming. As for conjunctural poverty, the hardships that befell those who normally had the ability and means to survive, it now resulted from the rhythms of international trade, culminating not only in worldwide economic slumps during the 1870s–1880s and the 1930s, but also in the dislocations that accompanied two world wars. As a result, an encounter with impoverishment became a commonly shared experience; people in diverse societies could trace their misery to the same economic events and dynamics. Industrialization and imperialism thus ensured that poverty around the globe, both the forms it assumed and the factors that triggered it, grew intricately intertwined with the operations of the world economy.

The increase in economic insecurity that grew out of this development is the primary focus of this chapter. Although its roots lay in the workings of global commerce, susceptibility to both structural and conjunctural poverty arose from different circumstances in industrial and dependent economies. In the first section, therefore, particular interest falls on the hardships resulting from both the process of industrialization itself and its social consequences, like urbanization. A subsequent section on dependent economies then focuses on the impacts of imperialism, especially the alienation of peasants from the land and their growing connection to a monetized economy. Together, both sections draw attention to the fact that although many causes of misery changed little over these years, like personal misfortune, harvest fluctuations, and overpopulation, the relationship between the world economy and revamped systems of resource allocation throughout the globe made poverty both less dangerous and more common.

Poverty in industrial economies

For industrial societies in particular, there is no question that poverty became less life-threatening during this period. Beginning with Great Britain, which first broke the limitations of an advanced organic economy, industrialized states amassed unparalleled wealth from what has been labeled a mineral-based energy economy. Coal, later oil and electricity, permitted the mechanization of manufacturing and transportation, which augmented stocks, reduced prices, and widened markets. Industrialization also restructured society, swelling the middling ranks that might fear poverty but seldom felt its pinch. Even the growing proletariat eventually benefited from improved conditions. As food prices declined, thanks in large part to shipments from such distant locales as Latin America and Australia, European workers saw their real wages increase noticeably. By the final decades of the nineteenth century, working-class families spent approximately half of their incomes on food, down almost 25 percent from earlier centuries. The "windfall" went to the purchase of mass-produced goods as varied as clothing and newspapers, and to the enjoyment of new leisure patterns growing up around music halls and cafés. Moreover, most family food budgets now commonly included items previously deemed luxuries, especially meat. At the same time, as societies prospered, so did states. Tax revenues supported larger bureaucracies and enhanced services. Officials gradually recognized that prosperity and defense rested partly on a healthy, educated population, and began to design social programs to reach that goal.

Although many in these societies might take solace in the fact that poverty rarely proved fatal by the middle of the twentieth century, it probably offered cold comfort to the growing number of men and women whose economic insecurity increased with industrialization. To some extent, this increased vulnerability resulted from the very nature of industrial capitalism and the process by which it was established. Before 1750, peasants and workers throughout the world benefited from either a direct connection to the land or a skill that increased the value of their labor. This tended to decrease their vulnerability to impoverishment. Industrialization changed that dynamic in striking ways. First, it decreased the proportion of the population making their living from farming. By the end of the nineteenth century, agriculture had ceded its economic prominence to manufacturing and an expanding service sector throughout Western Europe. The same occurred in Japan and the United States during the early decades of the twentieth century. More people thus survived from wage labor in factories, workshops, and retail stores. Second, mechanization, including the adoption of assembly-line techniques by the beginning of the twentieth century, decreased the skill required for even the most elaborate production practices. Many workers in manufacturing became "semi-skilled;" they acquired a limited skill in only one aspect of fabrication. In addition, that skill could typically be learned in a matter of hours or days. Finally, as mass production and consumption intensified, department stores and big business employed larger numbers of men and women as clerks. Like their counterparts on the factory floor, their limited skills in reading, writing, and arithmetic made them replaceable. Not only did labor thus become a commodity, but it also came to resemble a cog in a great machine. This significantly reduced the security of wage-laborers.

For individual workers, vulnerability rested in their expendability. And many employers were all too cognizant of this. Workers could lose their jobs, for example, if they ran afoul of new workplace regulations designed to instill discipline and increase productivity. Those who militated for unionization and better working conditions were particularly susceptible to such punitive action. They could also be blacklisted, making it almost impossible to find employment elsewhere. As for more desperate and docile workers, they were easily dispensable during periodic economic downturns – merely one more expense that needed to be trimmed. While guilds had theoretically maintained the centrality of extra-economic relations between the master and journeymen, industrial capitalism placed virtually no value on the bond between employer and employee. This was especially harmful to factory workers because new machinery increased their susceptibility to workplace accidents. Both the law and the prevailing economic logic usually cast the blame for such incidents on worker carelessness, leaving the employer free to discard the victim and engage the next willing job seeker. Finally, even when fully employed, the industrial workforce suffered from the "iron law of wages," a term coined by the British economic theorist David Ricardo in 1817. According to Ricardo, good business sense dictated that employers keep wages at bare subsistence. Higher wages would only increase the population, which would in turn drive wages back down. For many workers, then, full-time employment, on average ranging from 55 to 70 hours a week in late nineteenth-century Europe, made it extremely difficult to build a nest-egg in case of accident and illness.

Economic security was no less threatened outside of the workplace. Industrialization fostered urbanization, the concentration of the workforce and various services around factories and transportation centers. In highly industrialized countries like England and Germany, the percentage of urban residents equaled 80 percent and 70 percent respectively by 1950, up from less than 30 percent each in 1800. Both Japan and the United States also became roughly half urban by 1920. Unfortunately, few nations and cities could accommodate such growth. As it attracted textile factories, for example, the English village of Manchester grew from 17,000 inhabitants in 1750, to over 300,000 in 1853. Even well established cities expanded rapidly. Berlin grew from 500,000 in 1850 to 2 million in 1914, while metropolitan Tokyo's population rose from 2 million in 1900 to over 7 million in 1940. The result in many such areas was overcrowding and pollution. Besides having to pay high rents for cramped quarters, urban residents had to cope with open sewage in the streets and cesspits that typically mingled waste with drinking water. In mid-nineteenth-century Paris, for example, only eighty-two miles of sewers served a population of over 1 million people living along 250 miles of streets. Deadly epidemics, especially cholera, were common. In fact, until the twentieth century in Europe, urban growth resulted primarily from in-migration, not natural increase, for mortality remained dismally high in urban areas. In Bethnal Green, a section of East London, historians believe that life expectancy in the nineteenth century was two years lower than that estimated for Cro-Magnon man. Even if one managed to stay healthy enough to hold down a steady job, however, competition for housing ensured that affordable homes were scarce. In England, the state built over 1.5 million low-cost housing units during the interwar years and still could not meet demand. The expense of housing in a crowded market, as well as inadequate sanitation, combined to keep many industrial workers on the very edge of economic wellbeing.

The result for many workers was hardship in the form of structural poverty, especially during the early stages of industrialization. Although the economic data necessary to establish a decrease in workers' standards of living are inconclusive, the clearest evidence of long-term structural poverty among industrial workers arises from a rather surprising source, their heights. According to anthropometrics, stature reflects the amount of food available for a body's growth after essential maintenance needs have been met. So, a height differential between industrial workers and the rest of the population, especially rural workers, would indicate either that the former could not afford proper nutrition, particularly during key moments in adolescence and young adulthood, or that industrial labor required greater work effort at those same moments, leaving little nutrition beyond mainte- nance to support growth. And there is evidence that such a height differential opened up between urban and rural populations in both Western Europe and Japan as each experienced early industrialization. In Japan, for example, children's heights were stunted in urban areas before 1945, while growth rates during the post-1945 period indicate a significant improve- ment in the nutritional wellbeing of the working-class population once the early phases of industrialization had passed. Similarly, in Europe, workers' heights averaged several inches shorter than the bourgeoisie's. In fact, British concern with social welfare at the turn of the twentieth century was stimu- lated in part by the frail state of the working-class youths called up to fight the Boer War. So, even as conditions improved by the late nineteenth century, anthropometric data reveal that penury and malnutrition continued to color the existence of many in the expanding urban populations of indus- trial nations.

At the same time, those improving conditions contributed to feelings of impoverishment and vulnerability among the respectable poor and the lower middle classes that feared falling into their ranks. While they could afford to feed and shelter their families satisfactorily, the increased availability of consumer goods and a growing emphasis on consumption only served to highlight their social exclusion. Many of them could not keep pace with changing fashions and the latest trends, like the bicycle and daytrips to tourist destinations like Brighton and Blackpool. In addition, as owners of small workshops and retail stores, they felt the pressure of competing with expanding factories and department stores. For white collar workers, for example, meager wages made it difficult to maintain the proper outward appearance required by their employers, for workers who came into daily contact with the bourgeoisie had to resemble them, particularly in depart- ment stores. Many of them thus dressed like their employers, but had little left over to purchase the other accoutrements of a middle-class lifestyle, much to their frustration and shame. As for the lower middle class, many had no choice but to rely on married women's labor, even though doing so was a sure sign of working-class status. Indeed, so great was their fear of downward social mobility that the far-right political movements arising during the final decades of the nineteenth century had little difficulty attracting them as a core constituency. A similar dynamic squeezed the traditional elites who could not adapt to an industrial economy, such as the lesser nobility in Europe and the samurai in Japan. In short, then, the fluid social structure supported by industrialization led to the close connection of status and consumption. In this environment, even those who could support their immediate needs could feel deprived if their goals were to maintain appearances and to match certain social ideals. Though their poverty is difficult to compare to that of the workers living in squalor, their sense of vulnerability was no less real to them.

Industrialization also cemented the link between gender and poverty. First, employers and working-class men alike sought to preserve skilled positions, and the higher wages that went with them, for men. Of course, women did skilled labor, especially fine needlework, but society as a whole refused to define it as "skilled." Moreover, whenever possible, women were prohibited from learning how to use complex machinery, and machines continued to be built with male body dimensions in mind. The few times when employers sought to define equipment as "women's" machines, they did so to justify paying lower wages for those who would operate them. Such salary differentials were the second practice that made women more vulnerable to impoverishment. Men worked to support a family; women, even though they might be independent or widowed with dependent children, worked for "pin money." In fact, many early factories hired women precisely because they could pay them less and because they were more docile and easier to intimidate. This was especially true of the silk industry in Japan, which was notorious for reducing needy farm daughters to virtual slavery. Silk filatures often gave fathers an advance for their daughter's labor, and then paid the daughter almost nothing besides room and board. This effectively sentenced these young women to years of indentured servitude as they worked to pay off the advance. Records from one factory note that 10 of the 37 women employed there in 1919 actually owed the company money at the end of the year. Supporters of industrialization recognized that textile wages, earned predominantly by women, were low compared to salaries for similar work throughout the world, but they defended this by arguing that a cheap export item like silk was an essential ingredient for Japanese modernization. The profits would fund other necessary reforms. Third, women suffered from both the separation of productive from reproductive labor and the increased mobility prompted by industrialization. Many women and men could not afford to legalize their unions. This made it much easier for a man to desert his family, leaving the woman with little legal recourse. Moreover, whether married or not, women with children often faced the difficult task of finding childcare or accepting even lower wages doing "home-work." But even home-work became more difficult to find in the twentieth century. By

mechanizing and concentrating virtually all forms of manufacturing, factories made it almost impossible for many women to mix childcare and paid
labor. Among middle-class women, the cult of domesticity that restricted
them primarily to the home also limited their economic opportunities, justi-
fying legal double standards that made it increasingly difficult to function as
individual entrepreneurs. In this environment, urban markets housed an
ever-diminishing number of female-operated shops and stalls. Finally, the
sting of poverty often affected wives and mothers more directly, since they
were responsible for the daily tasks of feeding and clothing their families.
Susceptibility to structural poverty thus increased for women tied to the
industrial economy.

In the new conditions created by industrialization, the causes of conjunctural poverty, too, underwent dramatic transformation. Traditionally, harvest
failures were the most common source of economic downturns, even in
advanced organic economies. When crop yields declined, food prices
increased. As a result, household budgets included less leftover after meeting
the essential costs of food and shelter, adversely affecting manufacturing. As
markets shrank, employers reduced their workforce. Only better harvests
could end this downward cycle. With some variation in the particulars,
Western Europe experienced this cycle for the last time in the 1840s, when a
series of bad harvests led to hardship and helped set off the revolutions of
1848. In more mature industrial economies, however, capital flows and
market saturation drive economic cycles. Industrialization thrives on innovation. A larger share of the market belongs to the enterprise that can either
find a cheaper means of fabricating fashionable products or develop new
merchandise that captures popular attention. But achieving this requires
money to invest in, first, research and development and, second, implementation. Between 1750 and 1945, Western Europe's bourgeoisie invented a
number of institutions to supply that cash, from investment banks to corporations. As a result, economic health came to rest on the availability of
investment funds, i.e. capital. In this new scenario, a thriving economy has
many confident investors willing to speculate on future earnings, while an
ailing economy results from oversupplied markets and the resultant skittish-
ness of investors to gamble their money in schemes that seem unlikely to
reward risk with high dividends. Economists refer to the downsides of this
economic cycle as a recession, or, if long-lasting, a depression. Each of these
is marked by a restriction on credit, a decrease in production, and an increase
in unemployment, especially as employers try to cut the costs of their products in order to stimulate demand. Unfortunately, rising unemployment
reduces demand not only among those who no longer have jobs, but also
among those who fear that they, too, might soon see a dramatic decrease in
their incomes. As commerce decelerates, the rate of bankruptcies grows. In
the end, then, a depression means conjunctural poverty for unemployed
workers and insolvent employers, and a sense of vulnerability for everyone.

Economists typically reserve the term recession for short-term economic downturns with limited impacts, which tend to strike approximately every decade or so. Depressions, on the other hand, are more sustained and the misery is widespread. Between 1750 and 1945, the world experienced two such crises, each of which was labeled at the time the "Great Depression." The first occurred between 1873 and 1895, and reflected both the more effective integration of agricultural products from distant sources like Australia, and the rise of new industrial powers like Germany and the United States. Conditions were particularly harsh in the US, where over-speculation in the railroad led to the Panic of 1873 and the closure of the New York Stock Exchange for ten days. Between 1873 and 1876 over 17,000 businesses failed and unemployment reached 14 percent. The US economy began to bounce back in 1879, but depression conditions soon spread to Great Britain and France in the 1880s, when the textile industry suffered severe setbacks. Farming was also hard hit during these years, as the price of some grains fell 27 percent in France, 30 percent in the Netherlands, and 45 percent in England. This sparked a wave of migration to cities and overseas. In the end, it is possible to conclude that conjunctural poverty on the whole increased during this crisis as new technology, from refrigerated cargo ships and artificial fertilizers, to steel and petrochemicals, restructured the world economy. The second depression began in 1929 and lasted through the 1930s. It derived from weaknesses in international finance as a result of World War I, and from a maldistribution of income that resulted in overproduction and under-consumption. At its height in 1932–3, approximately one third of the US and 40 percent of the German labor force respectively was unemployed, and 25 percent of Englishmen were collecting unemployment benefits. Meanwhile, production throughout the industrial world, excluding the Soviet Union, declined by 37 percent. The Depression was particularly harmful for Germany and Japan, which depended on exporting manufactured goods to pay for short supplies of fuel and food. The value of Japanese exports fell by 50 percent between 1929 and 1931, for example, while the number of unemployed rose to 3 million. Although Japan's economy began to recover in 1931, the government achieved this by holding down wages in order to increase exports. As a result, real wages fell for Japanese workers. For politicians and workers alike, then, the Great Depression drove home an important lesson: poverty, whether structural or conjunctural, was firmly rooted in the operation of the world economy.

The only industrial nation to test that conclusion was the Soviet Union, which, because of its isolation, remained relatively immune to the Great Depression. At the same time, however, it demonstrates a final connection between poverty and industrialization. A mineral-based energy economy could strengthen a state to the extent that it could itself cause widespread economic hardship and vulnerability among its own population. Perhaps nothing illustrates that as clearly as Stalin's drive to complete industrialization in the 1930s. Under the tsars, Russia had initiated the process of mechanized manufacturing with some state assistance, but largely in private, often foreign, hands. By 1914, industrial capitalism had netted the nation a growing railroad network and factory districts principally around Moscow and St Petersburg. After the Revolution and Lenin's brief New Economic Policy, Stalin was determined to finish the process regardless of cost. To do this, he harnessed the power of both military force, which used modern weapons and could be dispatched easily along the rail lines, and propaganda, which reached the masses thanks to mechanized printing and the radio. Neither would have been possible before even limited industrialization. But the price of change was high. In order to collectivize the peasantry, for example, and liquidate the kulaks, Soviet officials deliberately instigated a deadly famine in 1932–3, causing the deaths of over 10 million people. For the survivors, many of whom became industrial workers, life was hard. Because the state guided Soviet industrialization, emphasis remained on heavy industry, not consumer goods. Moreover, its rapid pace resulted in drastic shortages in both housing and food, while the elimination of private trade in 1929 meant long lines and scarce stocks in state-run stores.

In Moscow, which was better provisioned than most of the Soviet Union, living standards plummeted. By 1937, the city's suburbs, for instance, which grew up overnight with virtually no municipal services like sewers and running water, were home to approximately 400,000 people. The numbers so overwhelmed city officials that they left the construction of much new housing to local industries, for these received better funding from the national government. Nonetheless, demand far exceeded supply. With one family per room, as many as fifteen families might live in one apartment, sharing a communal kitchen and bathroom. By 1935, the average housing per capita was only 4.2 square meters, despite a drop in fertility, itself a response to hardship. In the new industrial city of Magnitogorsk, conditions were even worse; mud huts still comprised 18 percent of housing in 1938. As for food, the government began to ration bread in Moscow in early 1929, followed shortly thereafter by such common items as sugar, butter, meat, and eggs. Rationing was extended to the entire country by the end of 1930. Shortages meant higher prices, but wages failed to keep pace. Real wages for Moscow's workers thus fell over one third between 1928 and 1937. In the end, while isolation from the world economy saved the Soviet Union from the increased conjunctural poverty that accompanied the Great Depression, state policies made structural poverty a way of life for millions of Russians. Privation was everywhere. John Scott, an American engineer, captured the differences between poverty in the Soviet Union and Western Europe well, when he described a trip to Paris in 1937 after spending five years in Magnitogorsk:

I went to a restaurant and bought the best chateaubriand in the house. While I was eating it, two able-bodied French working men, obviously unemployed, came around asking for alms. In all Russia you could not have found a piece of meat cooked and served as well as that chateaubriand, but you could have traveled the Soviet Union from one end to another and not found two able-bodied men anxious to work and unable to find a job. On the other hand the two French *chômeurs* were better dressed than most Russian skilled workers.

With all of its contradictions and hardships, that was the world that industrialization had created. More people around the globe now made their living from wage labor devoted to mass production and consumption. This left them vulnerable to the economic decisions of their employer, an often insalubrious environment, a volatile market, and a more powerful state. Conditions were often worse in the regions that we now call the non-developed world.

Poverty in the dependent economies

Imperialism ensured that the parts of the world that did not undergo industrialization were nonetheless thrown into turmoil by this significant transformation, for it is impossible to understand the former outside the context of the latter. Industrialization increased the demand for raw materials in places like Western Europe, Japan, and the United States, while providing them the technology for securing those resources regardless of indigenous desires. With their new-found power, they imposed an international division of labor that made the non-industrialized world the producers of less expensive raw materials and the consumers of foreign manufactured goods. To achieve this new imbalance, which left the rest of the world either directly or indirectly dependent upon industrialized nations and the vagaries of the world economy, imperialist powers destroyed traditional economic systems during the final decades of the nineteenth century and then set about creating new structures that better served their interests. Drawing the connection between industrialization and imperialism even tighter, some scholars have adopted a Marxist model for analyzing this development and portray the producers of primary export products as the world's proletariat. While there was no one path to that outcome, the result increased both poverty and vulnerability around the globe.

The process of devastating more or less independent economies typically began by impoverishing the states that protected the autonomy of their markets and systems of production. In some areas, like India and sub-Saharan Africa, Europeans achieved this via outright domination and displacement of traditional rulers. In regions where indigenous sovereigns retained at least nominal independence, like China and the Ottoman empire, industrialized nations used a combination of military might and indebtedness to achieve their goals. Usually, this entailed massive foreign loans for embattled sultans, pashas, and emperors who sought to retain control by embarking on their own expensive modernization projects. Unfortunately, when it became impossible to make payments, the industrial powers stepped in to enforce payment, often by demanding oversight of internal finances. This occurred, for example, in both Egypt and the Ottoman empire during the 1870s, and ended with British control of the Nile and the creation of the Ottoman Public Debt Administration in 1881, a European-dominated institution that oversaw Ottoman assets as a guarantee on debt. At times, when foreign interference sparked open opposition to imperial encroachment, indemnities added to the crushing weight of debt. In China, foreign loans and compensation payments for the Opium Wars and Boxer Rebellion simply overwhelmed the Qing dynasty. The inability to control their own tariff income, the product of the unequal treaties signed in the mid-nineteenth century, hindered the government even further, as did the creation of concession areas where Chinese leaders were powerless to tax the fortunes being made from foreign trade and development. In each of these regions, internal political decline or colonial rule had similar impacts: traditional safety nets for those in need, which typically rested on elite support, became less secure; entitlements underwent drastic alterations; and states proved ineffective in preventing the mass poverty that followed in the wake of imperialism.

Industrialized nations employed two principal strategies for reducing the viability of independent economies once encroachment began. The first, the alienation of native rights to natural resources, typically followed the assertion of colonial control. Often this was accomplished by forcibly removing indigenous populations. In Southern Rhodesia, for example, Europeans expropriated over 15 percent of the land, more than 16 million acres, within the first decade of colonization. In South Africa, in 1913, whites restricted African ownership of land to special reserves comprising only 13 percent of the territory. Since available land in these areas could not meet population growth, widespread poverty developed. Many had no choice but to move to urban slums in search of jobs or to contract themselves out to white farmers as either laborers or sharecroppers. Still others found punishing employment in the vast diamond and gold mines established in southern Africa. In other parts of sub-Saharan Africa, Europeans forced subsistence farmers off of the land by levying taxes. Since colonial officials assessed these by head and not on income, smallholders were hit hardest. Once they fell into debt, they had little choice but to sell their land. In many parts of East Africa, large plantations arose to take the place of smaller farms, while in other areas, commercial agriculture based on sharecropping became the norm. Latin America witnessed a similar dynamic, which displaced autonomous indigenous communities in places like Mexico and Argentina, where small-scale local commerce had previously coexisted with large commercial farms dependent on world markets. Of course, in Latin America, plantations were nothing new. Building on a solid foundation established between 1500 and 1750, creole elites expanded their control over vast stretches of land thanks to an influx of European and American capital after 1870. For a growing segment of the populations of both Latin America and sub-Saharan Africa, then, it became increasingly difficult to make a living outside of the world economy. Moreover, as we will see in greater detail below, new economic structures only enhanced people's susceptibility to poverty.

In civilizations with more integrated commercial economies and a fully developed manufacturing sector (in the forms of both urban crafts and cottage industry), imperialism triggered impoverishment by altering customary trading patterns and fostering deindustrialization, the second strategy for decimating traditional economic systems. West Africa once prospered from trans-Saharan trade, for example, but colonizers brought this to an end and reoriented markets toward the Atlantic. As for manufacturing, in 1750, India and China produced 24.5 percent and 32.8 percent of the world's manufactured goods respectively; by 1860 those figures had fallen to 8.6 percent and 19.7 percent and in 1913 they were 1.4 percent and 3.6 percent. During the same span of time, the industrial nations' share rose from 27 percent to 63.4 percent to 92.5 percent. In India, the decline in manufacturing, especially in textiles, was sparked by a wide range of factors. The consolidation of rule under the British, for example, shrank markets associated with the multiple royal courts that had divided India before the nineteenth century. At the same time, British control of customs and tariffs both at home and on the subcontinent allowed British textiles to flood the Indian market while pricing better quality Indian goods out of the British market. The British also altered India's internal market with public works schemes that stimulated greater demand for coarser British cloth among the lower castes, while enhancing their ability to reach more distant areas thanks to the railroads constructed in mid-century. Finally, the British put a great deal of effort into studying Indian designs and techniques, for Indian cloth was highly valued throughout the world. Only after copying Indian practices while reducing the price, for example, was Britain able to capture the textile market in the Ottoman empire in the 1850s. Of course, a commitment to world trade was a double-edged sword, especially when it pitted industrial powers against one another. Later, when inexpensive Japanese silk entered the market in the early twentieth century, both Indian and British shares of the market fell. By that time, the British economy was better able to absorb the shock, but Indian weavers once again suffered. Since textiles represented a significant portion of manufacturing well into the nineteenth century throughout the world, the ability of industrial nations to damage the spinning and weaving industries in places like India, the Ottoman empire, and China meant not only that those who remained in the craft had to accept lower standards of living in order to compete, but also that thousands would have to leave the profession, resulting in dramatic economic restructuring.

Once states and traditional economies had been decimated, imperialist powers then set about remaking foreign economies to suit their needs. These new economic systems generated high rates of both structural and conjunctural poverty, while leaving societies increasingly vulnerable as populations continued to grow and stretch beyond available resources. In some areas, like Latin America and parts of sub-Saharan Africa and Southeast Asia, the extraction of raw materials, both crops and minerals, became the mainstay of the economy. These export-driven systems attracted a great deal of capital from foreign investors and increased the overall productivity of these regions, giving the impression of economic growth per capita, but such appearances are deceptive. They hide tremendous income disparities, for the elites who operated these mines and estates maximized their profits by enforcing coercive labor patterns. Although outright slavery had ceased to be an option in much of the world once Western nations devoted their energies to ending the slave trade in the mid-nineteenth century, its replacement in many areas, debt peonage, was hardly better. This was a form of indentured servitude fostered by paying laborers in advance and forcing them to shop in "company stores" that charged exorbitant prices. Once indebted, the workers had no choice but to submit to low wages with no prospect of seeking other employment until the debt was paid – a virtual impossibility. Structural poverty became their lot in life. Even if they did manage to pay their debts, the growth of towns and cities stripped the countryside of practically all occupations outside of agriculture, making it more difficult to survive by cobbling together an "economy of makeshifts." To escape this cycle of poverty, one had to migrate to the city. Unfortunately, life was little better in urban areas, where scholars write of "proletarianization" and persistent low wages as causes of widespread poverty. A study of housing in Nairobi conducted in the late 1930s, for instance, discovered almost 500 men, women, and children living in accommodations designed for no more than 163. As in industrial societies, such poverty was also more prevalent among women. In many sub-Saharan African cultures, agriculture and commerce were within the female purview, but imperialist powers now limited women's activity. Moreover, European control of education and large-scale enterprises restricted women's occupations and opportunities. Finally, in areas that experienced widespread seasonal or temporary migration based on employment opportunities in mines, on plantations, or in new urban areas, the groups left behind consisted primarily of women and children, who were often forced to scratch out a meager existence on available resources and the little that male workers succeeded in sending home.

At the same time, because these economies relied upon a world market for inexpensive raw materials, their societies as a whole remained extremely vulnerable to conjunctural poverty, especially if agriculture had switched over to monoculture, or the specialization in one cash crop. An abundant harvest, for instance, risked flooding the market. Lower profits meant not only a potential drop in wages for laborers, but also decreased spending and hard times for the merchants who supplied the needs of workers and elites. The entire economy could suffer, as happened in Brazil during the 1890s when the overproduction of coffee led to depressed world markets. In addition, because international coffee-trading companies controlled the market, they could afford to buy surpluses at low prices during harvest and then sell their stocks when the prices began to climb, preventing the profits from ever reaching Brazilian pocketbooks. That is why scholars refer to the Latin American economy as "neocolonial" during the nineteenth and twentieth centuries; economic power and control resided outside the hands of these nominally independent nations. In essence, the economic difficulties experienced by coffee planters in Brazil differed little from those in the European colonies of East Africa. Conjunctural poverty also followed in the wake of the Great Depression of 1929, as crisis-stricken industrial economies dramatically cut back on their purchase of raw materials and agricultural commodities like coffee, sugar, and beef. In Latin America, the value of exports between 1930 and 1934 was only 48 percent of what it had been between 1925 and 1929. Meanwhile, sub-Saharan Africa experienced widespread unemployment for the first time in the 1930s. Despite plentiful resources, the continent's economy had been restructured to depend upon international markets, which could no longer support high demand. The Katanga copper mines in the Belgian Congo, for example, reduced their African workforce by over 60 percent between 1930 and 1933. At the same time, unemployment among able-bodied men reached 41 percent in Elizabethville (South Africa) and 25 percent in Nairobi (Kenya). In areas where monoculture had not yet become dominant, foodstuffs were still plentiful and relatively inexpensive, but this did little to alleviate the need for cash among the unemployed. In other areas, however, food was scarce, and attempts to diversify agriculture were hindered by the soil exhaustion caused by years of specialization in one main crop.

Even in areas less marked by dependence and large-scale farming and mineral extraction, imperialism spread impoverishment by encouraging widespread indebtedness. In some places, like the Ottoman empire, high taxes to pay the interest on foreign loans forced many peasants into share-cropping relationships based on cash advances for future harvests. While similar conditions, including a reorientation of agriculture to export markets, led to debt peonage and land concentration elsewhere, the availability of marginal land and the scarcity of labor, due to the high mortality from the empire's many wars during the nineteenth century, supported the proliferation of smallholdings among the Ottoman peasantry. In areas where landowners attempted to consolidate holdings and promote wage-labor on large estates, peasants either demanded high wages or migrated to areas where land was more available. In these conditions, elites decided that share-cropping was a more secure source of income. But the resulting low levels of productivity on small farms made it impossible for peasants to break out of debt, especially with usury rates running as high as 120 percent. Meanwhile, foreign competition with urban crafts made it impossible for poor peasants to seek opportunity in manufacturing. In the words of British envoy, Lewis Farley, in 1860:

> Turkey is no longer a manufacturing country. The numerous and varied manufactures which formerly sufficed, not only for the consumption of the empire, but which also stocked the markets of the Levant, as well as those of several countries in Europe, have in some instances, rapidly declined, and in others became altogether extinct. . . . There can be no doubt, therefore, entertained as to the possibility of an immense increase of the quantity of cotton grown in Turkey. . . . It is, in fact, this capa-bility of supplying raw material at a low price and of excellent quality which gives to Turkish commerce that importance and consideration in which it is held by the European powers.

Unfortunately, that "importance and consideration" rested on the impover-ishment of the Ottoman peasants, unable to plant and harvest enough to meet the overpowering burden of debt and taxes.

In many parts of China and India, smallholdings and sharecropping were also the norm, but this arose from overpopulation, not labor scarcity and an abundance of land. Between 1741 and 1850, the Chinese population grew 200 percent to 430 million people, but the amount of arable land grew by only 35 percent. While this alone led to peasant indebtedness, imperialism made conditions even worse. The outflow of silver initiated by the opium trade inflated the price of silver and skewed the silver/copper exchange system. In the eighteenth century, one tael of silver was worth 1,000 copper coins; by 1845 it was worth 2,000 copper coins. This hurt peasants who used copper as market currency, but had to pay taxes in silver. In essence, their tax burden doubled. Moreover, peasant tenants owed their rent in money, not in kind. And most landlords added property taxes to the rent, which could eventually reach as high as 60 percent of the crop yield. During the eighteenth century, many Chinese peasants were able to pay their bills only by participating in a thriving cottage industry, but this became more difficult in the nineteenth century, when competition from foreign goods destroyed cottage industry, first along the coasts and later, by the twentieth century, inland. While imperialist investment in the cities and concession areas gave rise to some employment opportunities, overpopulation kept wages low. The rise of the Guomindang (or Nationalist) government in the 1920s made some improvements in urban economic conditions, particularly

once the Chinese government regained tariff autonomy by 1929 and began
to recover concession areas in the 1930s, but this made little difference to
the overwhelming majority of Chinese peasants, approximately 80 percent of
the population, who languished in poverty in the countryside. According to
a League of Nations study of South China, tenant and semi-tenant farming
accounted for 60–90 percent of all agriculture, with occupants paying
between 40 and 60 percent of the annual crop in rent. In this environment,
structural poverty and indebtedness were so pervasive that traditional clan-
based relief mechanisms began to break down.

Similar conditions developed in colonial India. However, the rise of
smallholdings and widespread indebtedness arose more from what some
historians describe as a "peasantization" of Indian society during the nineteenth century, when the decline of older internal market and bureaucratic
centers led those who had once made their livings in commerce and crafts to
turn to the land as the sole source of income. In the scramble for land, landlords began to raise rents and push more of the costs for upkeep onto the
tenants. Meanwhile, as Indian capital no longer generated surpluses outside
of agriculture, the economy soon mutated, leading Indian elites to emphasize squeezing the peasant economy as much as possible as a prime source of
enrichment. Very little attention went to investment and entrepreneuri-
alism. For their part, those who remained in urban crafts, like weavers who
specialized in luxury cloth, were forced to lower both their standards of
living and their own production costs in order to survive. The latter required
them to purchase factory-made materials, like machine-spun yarn, which
then increased their indebtedness to the middlemen who sold such
commodities. Like sharecroppers, buying items necessary to production
forced these craftsmen to borrow on the anticipated value of the finished
product. One miscalculation in the price of either raw materials or
completed merchandise could thus result in often debilitating debt. In the
end, the Indian economy, like its Chinese and Ottoman counterparts, proved
unable to stimulate the mass purchasing power that might have led to
economic development, a situation that the Great Depression of 1929 only
made worse. Instead, poverty became the norm.

Conclusion

In the history of world poverty, the balance sheet for the period between
1750 and 1945 is somewhat mixed. As the world economy intensified, it
integrated far more of the globe's population into one "world system." This
caused fewer people to experience poverty as a brush with death. Instead,
industrialized societies enjoyed unprecedented economic growth, while, even
in the poorest regions, famine mortality fell dramatically as a result of better
transportation and a more responsive market. Although this would later lead
to overpopulation and increased poverty in some places, like sub-Saharan

Africa, this was not a grave concern before 1945. However, these developments only changed the nature of poverty, they did not eliminate it. In the
more prosperous manufacturing economies, mass markets spawned increased
rates of relative poverty by the dawn of the twentieth century. Though many
in the working classes remained malnourished and more prone to illness, a
growing number of people now felt poor because they could not afford to
participate fully in the ever-evolving consumer economy. In agricultural
societies, a rising dependence on the market for food and other necessities,
compounded by specialization in cash crops and widespread indebtedness,
transformed poverty into chronic malnutrition. Staple crops, even in abundance, could not make up for the diverse essentials of a healthy diet, and
much of those were too expensive for many people to incorporate regularly
into their daily regimen.

But, while poverty became less life-threatening, it also became more
widespread. So did the sense of vulnerability that made impoverishment a
constant concern. In industrial societies, the mechanization of manufacturing and a growing service sector reduced many to wage labor, yet the
labor market was rarely lucrative and secure enough to insulate workers and
consumers from hardship and insecurity. With the additional burdens of
unsanitary conditions in expanding cities and a housing shortage that made
safe accommodation scarce and expensive, structural poverty, even though
relative in nature, became a common condition, especially for the many
female workers discriminated against by prevailing gender norms. Severe
upsurges in conjunctural poverty caused by the great depressions that
followed the crises of 1873 and 1929 only exacerbated the situation.
Ironically, though the Soviet Union could rightfully claim immunity to such
economic downturns, it also demonstrates that industrialized economies
could support much stronger states capable of reducing their entire populations to penury. Among the world's dependent economies, conditions were
even worse. Using the tools of land expropriation and unequal trade regulations, imperialist powers reduced many societies to a challenging existence
as suppliers of raw materials and markets for cheap manufactured products.
In regions as diverse as South Asia, sub-Saharan Africa, Latin America, the
Middle East, and China, similar positions in world trade engendered almost
permanent indebtedness among both states and their populations. Though
the exact causes of individual impoverishment could vary from debt peonage
to high taxation, from inflated usury rates to exorbitant rents, most of the
poor in these dependent economies could trace their hardships back to the
operations of the world economy.

Amidst such dramatic changes, however, some noteworthy features of
world poverty persisted. The link between impoverishment and age, for
example, strengthened as the practice of wage labor spread. Children and the
elderly, who were dependent upon the earning potential of others, remained
particularly vulnerable. Before the implementation of Social Security in

1935, over half of all senior citizens in the United States lived in poverty. For children, their fortunes were frequently tied to another group who bore a disproportionate share of economic insecurity, women. Gender biases, in the forms of both informal prejudices and legal limitations, continued to mark women as more vulnerable to structural and conjunctural poverty. In commercial and monetized economies throughout the world, many women experienced need as both earners and consumers; receiving lower salaries than men, enjoying fewer opportunities for gainful employment, and facing the daily task of stretching limited resources to feed and clothe their families. Likewise, imperialism only heightened the prominence of race as another marker of poverty. As the West's wealth and power increased, so too did susceptibility to economic hardship in the rest of the world.[1] This dynamic was particularly stark in areas colonized by Europeans, like India and sub-Saharan Africa, where white plantation owners, traders, and colonial officials grew rich as native populations saw their prospects diminish. In the Americas, despite the end of slavery, racial prejudices mirrored the impacts of gendered double standards to keep most African Americans, indigenous peoples, and mestizos in precarious economic arrangements like debt peonage and sharecropping. In the end, then, many of the prevailing patterns of impoverishment already evident in world history before 1750 solidified in the wake of a global economy fueled by industrialization and imperialism.

As we will see in the following chapters, the growing recognition that insecurity and want were natural by-products of that world economy gradually led elites around the globe to reconsider traditional attitudes toward charity and social welfare. At first, this prompted leaders in the wealthier industrial societies to devise intricate programs to cope with the insecurity of the labor market and the vagaries of life in a market economy. This is the subject of Chapter 5. After 1945, however, the emphasis shifted to international strategies that finally acknowledged how fiscal policies in one region could dramatically alter living conditions halfway around the world. Along with the changing dynamics of world trade after the Second World War, the resulting development plans and institutions are the focus of Chapter 6.

Further reading

On industrialization and its social impacts: Steven M. Beaudoin, *The Industrial Revolution* (Boston MA: Houghton Mifflin, 2003); Sheila Fitzpatrick, *Everyday Stalinism* (New York: Oxford University Press, 1999); Mikiso Hane, *Peasants, Rebels, and Outcastes: The Underside of Modern Japan* (New York: Pantheon Books, 1982); David L. Hoffmann, *Peasant Metropolis: Social Identities in Moscow, 1929–1941* (Ithaca NY: Cornell University Press, 1994); and Peter N. Stearns, *The Industrial Revolution in World History* (Boulder CO: Westview Press, 1993). On dependent economies: Peter

Harnetty, " 'Deindustrialization' Revisited: The Handloom Weavers of the Central Provinces of India, c. 1800–1947," *Modern Asian Studies* 25, 3 (1991): 455–510; John Ilife, *The African Poor* (New York: Cambridge University Press, 1987); Huri Islamoglu-Inan, *The Ottoman Empire and the World Economy* (New York: Cambridge University Press, 1987); Resat Kasaba, *The Ottoman Empire and the World Economy: The Nineteenth Century* (Albany NY: SUNY Press, 1988); Rosemary Thorp, *Progress, Poverty and Exclusion: An Economic History of Latin America in the 20th Century* (Baltimore MD: Johns Hopkins University Press, 1998); D. A. Washbrook, "Progress and Problems: South Asian Economic and Social History c. 1720–1860," *Modern Asian Studies* 22, 1 (1988): 57–96.

Chapter 5

Poverty, morality, and the state, 1750–1945

In 1913, a young, though already much accomplished, Albert Schweitzer arrived in Lambaréné, French Equatorial Africa (now Gabon) determined to devote his considerable talents to alleviating the misery he saw all around him. Trained as a philosopher, theologian, musician, and physician, he gained worldwide fame as a medical missionary who had given up a promising career in Europe to live out the rest of his life assisting the poor of sub-Saharan Africa, both directly by nursing the sick and needy, and indirectly by fixing the world's attention on the plight of the continent's poor. Although, to a certain extent, his experiences followed a path well trod by the many Christian missionaries who had traveled to sub-Saharan Africa since the fifteenth century, his life and philosophy also represent one aspect of a significant transformation in prevailing attitudes toward poverty and its relief throughout much of the world between approximately 1880 and 1945. Schweitzer based his assistance not on the promise of adding more souls to the ranks of the world's Christians, but on what he termed "the Fellowship of those who bear the Mark of Pain." In other words, the affluent who had experienced suffering in their lives had a duty to ease the pain of those less fortunate without recompense. Schweitzer expected little from his patients. He saw them neither as heathens in need of spiritual solace first and foremost, nor as "noble savages" who carried some essential lesson for corrupted civilizations. And he was not alone in adopting this approach. As the Irish nun Marie Helena Martin explained when she founded the Medical Missionaries of Mary Catholic order in 1937:

> Medical Mission work presupposes doing physical good to all who ask us – as Our Blessed Lord did. The question of conversion or change of life may come later. . . . It is not for us to go out preaching the Gospel – although we are always ready to answer our patients' enquiries – we pave the way for the acceptance of Our Lord's teaching.

In essence, the moral reform component to poor relief receded. To the extent that charitable donors sought to alter behavior among the poor, the lessons focused on scientific knowledge that would curb disease and hunger. As one scholar expressed it, Schweitzer was thus a "vital bridge" between traditional charity and modern secular relief.

Before this transition, attitudes toward poverty and charity in many of the world's civilizations were deeply embedded in conceptualizations of morality and spirituality. In some areas, indigence reflected the stains of indolence and contamination; in others, assistance was a moral obligation that defied easy systemization because it was intended to achieve salvation for the donor while strengthening individual reputations and building bonds of patronage. Even in Western Europe, where much of poor relief had been secularized and standardized between 1450 and 1750, popular belief continued to see misery, particularly among the able-bodied, as the product of moral failings. Consequently, benefactors took great pains to assess the worthiness of relief recipients and typically coupled assistance with the expectation of reform. At first, industrialization and imperialism did little to alter this, despite an escalating vulnerability to impoverishment in most societies and the increasing difficulty of maintaining traditional relief practices. In England, for example, a drastic overhaul of existing poor laws in 1834 produced a draconian system that enshrined the belief that generous public assistance weakened the moral fiber of the nation and gave rise to lazy and feckless workers. Meanwhile, European missionaries placed a higher premium on religious conversion than assistance. Christian doctors in Africa and Asia were actively discouraged from treating gravely ill patients who might not recover, for their deaths would deter others from adopting the new faith. Gradually, however, the long-established link between morality and religion, on the one hand, and poverty and its relief on the other, eroded after 1880 (although it has never disappeared completely). A growing number of aid workers throughout the world rejected the argument that indigence was either a necessary and permanent part of life or a punishment for sloth and improper behavior. They began to argue, instead, that misery arose from the operation of the economy, poor sanitary conditions, and a lack of education. Like Schweitzer and Marie Martin, they also cast off the traditional link between assistance and moral reform. As a result, many advocated for a more comprehensive and "scientific" approach to poor relief, one that pushed beyond emergency relief for the conjunctural poor and private initiative for the destitute. In their eyes, only the state, or at the least, large, centralized relief organizations, could undertake such an enormous task, and the decades before 1945 witnessed many attempts to construct just such programs and associations.

This chapter examines both the causes of that transition and its impacts, especially the origins of the welfare state and new relief organizations. It is important to note at the start, however, two essential aspects of that transformation. First, in a broad sense, industrialization and imperialism set its foundations, for it was possible only to the extent that poverty had become less life-threatening. As both the wealth and reach of industrialized nations grew, famine deaths declined around the globe. In industrialized areas, where relative poverty became the norm, as in colonial societies, where Westerners accepted the responsibility to prevent starvation and new transportation technology limited the impacts of natural disasters, reformers were free to widen their concern for the destitute and conjunctural, or crisis, poor to include the structural poor. Moreover, the spread of science established a paradigm that made social problems like poverty liable to human solutions. Second, shared origins did not necessarily translate into shared outcomes. The paths that led to more systematized poor relief in many regions of the world were marked by tremendous diversity and uneven results. In sub-Saharan Africa, for example, colonial governments, the strength of traditional attitudes toward poverty, and the dislocations caused by imperialism all combined to weaken the impacts of these new attitudes. Schweitzer's innovations were slow to catch on. Meanwhile, in Turkey, reformers heralded state social welfare as a central component of modernization and state formation, while innovations in Japanese public assistance succeeded only because they could be promoted as natural outgrowths of Confucianism and imperial governance. Similarly, in Western Europe and the Soviet Union, the wide range of state-supported programs established before 1945 reflected the significant role of internal politics and traditions in shaping the contours of the welfare state. Despite this jumble of motives and results, one central point remains. Starting in the final decades of the nineteenth century, more and more of the world's population came to see poverty, especially among the able-bodied, as a societal scourge demanding concerted attention. As such, it became a suitable concern for public discourse, and an apt agenda for the state.

New outlooks on poverty and relief

The most dramatic shifts in attitudes toward poverty and relief occurred primarily among the industrialized societies of the world before 1945. In these regions, even structural poverty lost much of its stigma and effective aid fell largely within the state's expanding purview. The old ideas were tenacious, however. In Meiji Japan, heightened concern over economic misery produced a Relief Regulation of 1874 that continued to restrict state assistance to the destitute, for example. Although the legislators who enacted this new law now accepted the argument that poverty was not natural and inevitable, and thus required government action, they maintained the traditional view that the able-bodied poor were somehow tainted by moral weakness and should thus rely solely on family and community networks. In England, too, the poor law reform of 1834 firmly established the concept of "less eligibility" as the foundation for public assistance. According to this doctrine, subsistence wages were the only way to prevent rampant over-population and indolence among the working class. Therefore, monetary relief, which was to be avoided whenever possible in favor of the workhouse, should never match the lowest wages earned by an independent worker in the community regardless of family size and the cost of living. Otherwise, workers would opt for relief and cease to be productive. In many areas, such beliefs found firm support in the success of liberalism, a political, social, and economic doctrine that emphasized the rights of the individual over community ties and state regulation. Consequently, charity and self-help associations stood alone as the most effective means of alleviating poverty. According to Adolphe Thiers, a leading French liberal in the nineteenth century, charity, a private virtue, had to remain "voluntary, spontaneous, free to be or not be," even when it became public,

> for otherwise, it would cease to be a virtue and become a constraint and a disastrous one. If an entire class could demand instead of receive, it would take on the role of a beggar who asks with a rifle in his hand.

Such attitudes began to change in the 1880s, however, for myriad reasons. First, as industrial economies continued to develop, new causes of poverty such as increased dependence on wage labor and distant markets became more evident. In the wake of the Great Depression of 1873, in particular, middle-class reformers in the West began to realize that large sectors of the population had no other source of survival than the sums they earned from selling their labor, a risky proposition in an age of impersonal business cycles. In Japan, similar concerns arose not just from poor living conditions among the working class, but also from indigence among the samurai who failed to find a place in the new social and economic order. Second, the rise of the social sciences, especially the social survey, further reshaped elite ideas about poverty. Pioneered in Britain by Henry Mayhew, Charles Booth, and Seebohm Rowntree in the last decades of the nineteenth century, social surveys mapped the presence of poverty in England's major cities and added a statistical dimension to popular views that typically linked poverty to immorality and even criminality. By integrating data on wages, rents, and food prices into their surveys, these social scientists were able to demonstrate that much poverty arose from low wages and that many poor families struggled to maintain the trappings of respectability despite their misery. Last, these data took on a more human face thanks to the rise of the mass press, expanded literacy, and the journalistic technique of the exposé. Journalists like W. T. Snead in London helped to humanize the poor and draw greater attention to their troubles. As a result of all of this, elites in Europe, Japan, and the United States began to appreciate that structural poverty was not necessarily the result of moral failings but of impersonal economic forces.

In addition to new opinions on poverty and its causes, many in these societies also began to rethink the best means of assisting the poor. In particular, enhanced systems of state-supported social welfare became much more acceptable. Here, too, historians emphasize multiple causes for the shift, but these could differ among specific societies. In Japan, for example, supporters of public assistance emphasized its roots in Confucianism and the traditional solicitude the emperor maintained for his subjects. It is no surprise, therefore, that while other "progressive" ideologies that underscored deficiencies in Japanese society, like democracy, unionism, and liberalism, were typically denounced as foreign and suppressed by the government, petitions for increased state welfare met with success in 1929 and 1932. Meanwhile, in Europe and the United States, Progressivism, or Solidarism, challenged the reigning assumptions of liberalism at the turn of the century by promoting the concept of social solidarity. In the eyes of progressive reformers, the dangers posed by poverty and national decline for the entire community outweighed the supposed risks of welfare for the individual worker's moral character. At the same time, the new scientific dimension to the problem of poverty fostered the belief that it could be solved by the systematic application of the scientific method. These ideas came together most prominently in the West in a new concern for maternalist welfare in the 1880s. More common to all of the world's societies were the impacts of nationalism and Social Darwinism, which also denied the primacy of the individual. Nationalism emphasized the needs of the national community, while Social Darwinism argued that the weakness of some segments of the population could hinder the ability of the whole to compete successfully against other nations in the struggle for survival. In their own ways, each of these doctrines thus supported a great role for the state in securing the needs of its citizens. Finally, some historians argue that state-supported social welfare became easier to contemplate once reformers adapted the actuarial logic of insurance to society as a whole in the 1890s.

Perhaps the most important reason for these transformations in attitudes, however, was the rise of socialism and working-class radicalism, for these were at the heart of what was popularly known as "the social question" in most industrialized societies. Already at the turn of the nineteenth century, French radicals had begun to argue for a far more equitable distribution of society's wealth. Such views spread quickly in industrialization's wake. While early socialists like Charles Fourier and Robert Owen believed that equality of condition could be achieved peacefully, this approach was eclipsed in mid-century by more hard-line socialists and anarchists who argued that such transformations could only be won through bloodshed. Though the movement also spawned legal and nonviolent political parties no less devoted to an egalitarian economic system, it was the violent rhetoric that often seized attention. Thanks to the rise of the mass press and new technology that united the world via a web of foreign correspondents, news of assassinations at the hands of anarchists, of electoral successes by fledgling socialist parties, and of widespread strikes and labor stoppages, mesmerized an increasingly literate population. In the United States, for example, the middle classes grew increasingly alarmed by the 1877 national rail strike, the 1886 Haymarket Square bombing and riot in Chicago, and the assassination of President William McKinley in 1901. Across the Atlantic, the situation seemed just as ominous. Britain's first national walkout had been unsuccessful in 1898, but a new wave of strikes erupted in most of the nation's major cities again between 1910 and 1912. In France, 1904 alone saw more than 1,000 strikes, while in Germany, the Socialist Party, the SPD, had firmly established itself as the main opposition party in the Reichstag by 1914. Though the situation remained far calmer in Japan, there, too, the press raised fears by highlighting the rise of urban poverty in the late 1880s and 1890s. Concerns only deepened throughout the world once the Bolsheviks seized power in Russia in 1917 and German radicals launched their own failed revolution in the aftermath of World War I. It is ironic, therefore, that state-supported assistance often opened up rifts among socialists, with hardliners arguing that such palliatives only delayed the inevitable revolution. Nevertheless, in this atmosphere, many reformers began to tout social welfare and social insurance as viable means of integrating the disaffected working class into the existing capitalist system. These programs would have the added benefit of strengthening the health of the nation just when it seemed that the struggle for survival was at its height.

Even in societies without large populations of industrial workers, widespread beliefs about poverty and its relief were also undergoing scrutiny and revision. In the Moslem world, for example, where charity was a religious duty, both proponents and opponents of various regimes politicized poor relief by making it a tool of statecraft. This isn't surprising given the dislocations caused by imperialism and the desperate scramble by many leaders to demonstrate their worth as protectors of the needy and vulnerable, while staving off challenges to their rule from within and without. In Ottoman Turkey, one way that mid-nineteenth-century reformers attempted to weaken the Sultan's personal power was to bureaucratize alms-giving, which had previously served as basis for a vast system of patronage. When Sultan Abdulhamid II (r. 1876–1909) sought to revive his personal rule, therefore, his strategy included using practices like weekly distributions of charity after Friday services at the Hamidiye mosque in Constantinople to legitimize his regime according to Islamic traditions, and to portray himself as a benevolent and paternal Sultan beloved by his poor subjects. The "Young Turks" who seized power in 1908 dismantled this system and replaced it with a municipally based program funded by a specific line in the public budget, not the Sultan's household. In Egypt, on the other hand, the Khedive led the way in systematizing assistance in the 1830s and 1840s, especially by prohibiting begging in the streets of Cairo and Alexandria, the only cities with official shelters to house the needy. In this manner, he bureaucratized relief by establishing the police department, or Dabtiyya, to serve as an intermediary between those arrested for begging and the destitute they deemed "deserving" of assistance from the state. The able-bodied, especially rural immigrants, typically failed to qualify since Egypt's government required their labor, either in the military or in agricultural monopolies and fledgling industries meant to fund the nation's modernization. Although built on traditional values and less regulated and standardized than developments in Europe and Japan, these new directions in poor relief diminished the role of individual charity as a system of patronage while increasing the role of the state as an impersonal purveyor of aid.

In addition to increased government assistance, a dramatic growth in the number and size of charitable organizations in many regions of the world also captured changing attitudes toward poverty and assistance during these years. In Russia, where public assistance was particularly weak, private initiative struggled to pick up the slack as the question of poverty rose in prominence. An early twentieth-century survey of these charities indicates that approximately 60 percent had been established in the 1890s. Over half of these Russian associations specialized in specific populations, like needy students, a trend that characterized philanthropy in other parts of the world, too. By joining state officials in standardizing and bureaucratizing aid, many of these organizations moved beyond traditional benevolent societies that emphasized individual initiative, irregular distributions, and the morality of both donors and beneficiaries. Instead, they adopted goals of organized collective action for both assistance and social, not moral, reform. In Egypt, for example, the Society of Egyptian Ladies' Awakening, founded around 1920, emphasized education for poor women and girls, not because recipients lacked proper values of thrift and hard work, but because they were not prepared to prosper in Egypt's changing economy. In this respect, its actions represented a significant departure from the Islamic traditions enshrined in *zakat* and the *waqf*. In a similar vein, many of the maternal aid societies that sprang up in Europe during the late nineteenth century also emphasized a more scientific training for mothers of young children, though moral lessons were hard to abandon completely. Some charities, for instance, refused assistance to those who could not prove the legitimacy of their children. Such attitudes became harder to maintain, however, as European culture became secularized. Reliant on public donations, these charities found it in their best interests to assume a neutral tone on religious and political issues.

One final indicator of changing views on poor relief is the evolving relationship between the state and voluntary associations in many societies, a clear sign of the continued politicization of the issue. Some of these organizations, like England's Charity Organization Society, grew out of a desire to forestall growth in state assistance. The men and women who founded this organization in 1869 accepted the liberal faith in small government and argued that enhanced charitable activity was the ideal solution for the social question. Other groups arose to meet new needs defined by changing state policies, and often took a lead in lobbying politicians to expand public assistance and social welfare. In France, legislation passed in 1889 granted the state the power to remove children from unfit homes, prompting the creation of private charitable institutions designed specifically to house these new wards of the state. Five years later, reformers established a new association in Paris known as the Musée Social, a think tank designed not only to study the pressing social and economic issues of the day, but also to push politicians into following their lead. Some countries, like Russia, even facilitated the formation of new charities by publishing model charters, which was especially important in regions where associations still required government authorization. Of course, relations between such groups and public officials were not always cordial. In Egypt, for example, organizations like The Future of the Nation and the Society of Egyptian Ladies' Awakening fed off nationalist discontent and a nascent civil society. A new middle class resented European claims that the throngs of impoverished in Cairo's streets signaled the continuing need for imperialist "tutelage," while also growing fearful that traditional leaders were incapable of preventing the potential unrest that might arise from widespread poverty. This in turn spurred the Egyptian government to emphasize its own effectiveness and to police charitable organizations that solicited funds by publicizing their success and efficiency. In 1939, this culminated in the creation of the Ministry of Social Affairs, which touted official solicitude while barring charities from engaging in political activity. Officials were particularly eager to contain the activities of both communists and the Muslim Brotherhood, both concerned with assisting the poor as part of far-reaching plans for social and political change.

Between 1880 and 1945, virtually all of the world's societies thus experienced significant transformations in traditional attitudes about poverty and poor relief. Much, though not all of this can be traced both directly and indirectly to the impacts of industrialization and imperialism. In particular, new economic practices, governing structures, and cultural patterns all challenged long-established links between morality and poverty. For many, abolishing need and want became the legitimate ends of collective action spearheaded by the state. Given the mixture of motives and participants involved in this debate, however, these changing outlooks rarely produced uniform results.

Social welfare, social insurance, and organized relief

Unsurprisingly, the most noteworthy result of new ideas about poor relief was a tremendous growth in state assistance. This was most evident in the various programs devised by European politicians to alleviate structural poverty among workers and to promote the health and welfare of large segments of the population. Though their development was uneven and followed different paths among most states, taken as a whole they represent the antecedents of what would become known as the welfare state after 1945. Of course, the wealth required for such undertakings remained primarily in the coffers of those countries that had undergone significant industrialization before the Second World War: Japan, the United States, the Soviet Union, and most of the nations of Western Europe. In the rest of the world, despite a growing belief that the state should constitute a major bulwark against deprivation, some combination of insufficient funds and colonial neglect typically left local officials powerless to expand relief beyond meager aid for the destitute and emergency care for the conjunctural poor. Even in those regions without significant public assistance, however, the years between 1880 and 1945 witnessed the early foundation of more organized efforts at poor relief in the hands of large-scale benevolent societies. Like the welfare state, the widespread development of international relief agencies would have to await the decades after 1945, but the seeds were sown by men like Albert Schweitzer before then. In the final analysis, then, these years experienced the beginnings of an important shift in what some scholars have labeled the mixed economy of relief; while industrialization and imperialism eroded the usefulness of traditional sources of survival such as begging, the informal economy and community networks, new possibilities were gradually developing to take their place.

In nations where state assistance increased dramatically, most new programs fell into one of two major categories: social insurance or social welfare. Social insurance was the most innovative approach to poverty, though many deemed it acceptable principally because it rested on a traditionally liberal foundation of individual thrift. The goal was to insure workers against foreseeable causes of impoverishment, like illness and old age, by created state-managed funds amassed through contributions by workers, employers, and the state itself. The primary objective was thus to prevent penury among workers and, through them, their families. Note, however, that formulating programs in this manner privileged male workers. In the vast majority of social insurance programs women received benefits only as wives or widows of insured men. Initially, most states began such insurance schemes with very limited goals – they wanted to guarantee the viability of these funds by limiting the pool only to well paid, skilled workers. The most commonly insured "risks" were workplace accidents, inability to work due to old age, and sickness. Here, Germany led the way. Between 1883 and 1889, the new German state created compulsory contributory schemes to fund up to thirteen weeks of relief if sick or injured, expanded to twenty-six weeks in 1903. As for old age pensions, these were available once workers turned seventy. Other states soon followed suit. Britain had a comparable range of programs by 1911, France by 1930, and the United States began to move in a similar direction with the implementation of Franklin Roosevelt's New Deal in the 1930s. In 1911, Britain also ventured onto less secure terrain with compulsory unemployment insurance. This generated much more opposition than the other schemes because the business cycle that periodically raised unemployment rates represented an actuarial risk that was much harder to predict with any accuracy, unlike sickness and old age. Moreover, to many critics, it was a classic example of a "moral hazard." In other words, paying the unemployed raised the possibility of "corrupting" them so that they stopped looking for work. In addition, they argued, no state could guarantee the feasibility of unemployment insurance during periods of crisis, as the world would discover during the Great Depression of the 1930s. The British tried to account for this by linking benefits to labor exchanges, or unemployment offices, which tested the willingness to work, and by implementing waiting periods and limits on the duration of benefits. Nevertheless, this was the one insurance program that did not spread across Europe as quickly before 1920.

During the interwar years, social insurance gradually expanded to cover new groups like white collar workers, the self-employed, and farm workers. Sometimes this legislation created national funds; more often, the state oversaw separate accounts for the various social categories. As much as possible, reformers took great pains to assure critics that the expansion of these programs would protect society against the harmful effects of poverty without altering the social balance. First, whatever money taxpayers contributed to insurance funds via state subsidies would be offset by savings from a decrease in the numbers of poor families collecting public assistance. Second, in nations where private mutual aid societies had flourished during the nineteenth century, like France, legislators were careful to integrate these associations into the operation of government programs. Finally, these schemes were never meant to be redistributive. As other groups entered the system, public officials created separate endowments with separate levels of compensation. So, industrial workers received different benefits than white collar workers, who received different benefits than farm workers. Social insurance was truly meant to decrease vulnerability to impoverishment, not to raise standards of living through the redistribution of society's wealth.

Social welfare, the second category of new programs, came closest to approximating older efforts to aid the poor. Unlike social insurance, it was aimed chiefly at those who stood outside of the labor market, i.e. those who could not work because of infirmity or age. The major differences with previous endeavors were the systemization of relief under government oversight, the expansion of programs thanks to the support of public revenue, and the establishment of legal rights to assistance. Many of these programs remained means-tested, however, like the pensions for the infirm and elderly legislated for in France in 1905 and in Britain in 1908. For some historians, broad-based public health measures also fall under the rubric of social welfare, like the new sanitation and housing regulations established in most of Europe's major cities in the late nineteenth century. Free meals and medical exams for school children seconded this undertaking. The most innovative programs, however, attempted to shift some of what scholars refer to as the costs of social reproduction away from individual families and toward society as a whole. In essence, employers pay wages only for labor and do not concern themselves with employees once they have left the workplace. Moreover, during most of the nineteenth century, industrialists insisted that employment contracts were negotiated among individual workers and companies. As a rationale for opposing collective bargaining this was a chief union-busting technique. All of this passes the cost of raising families and providing new generations of workers (i.e. social reproduction) onto the workers themselves. Many of them may have argued for a "family wage," but employers never made distinctions in pay according to the marital and family status of individual employees. At the same time, nationalism and Social Darwinism began to convince many that they depended literally upon the health of their populations and on the nation's ability to maintain the supply of workers. So, reformers placed increased emphasis on using the state to help meet the costs of social reproduction, especially when it came to ensuring the health and numbers of future generations.

The result was a host of new programs to promote maternal and infant health and welfare. Because of their concern with depopulation and a falling birth rate, made particularly alarming by population growth in neighboring Germany, the French pioneered this form of social welfare in the late nineteenth century with the creation of publicly funded health clinics for pre-natal care, childbirth, and infant care, as well as family allowances for needy families with four or more children. The state also supported maternity leaves both before and after birth. With a small population, French politicians recognized that they would never be able to convince mothers to stay home and have more children; women's paid labor outside the home was necessary to both working-class families and the nation's economic health. Therefore, they had to make it easier for working women to work *and* have children. This logic soon resonated in other European nations as well. By 1914, France, Luxembourg, Germany, Switzerland, and Austria-Hungary all had legally enforced, paid maternity leaves following the birth of a child, while only France and Switzerland alone offered such leaves before childbirth, too. Great Britain, Portugal, Norway, the Netherlands, and Belgium, on the other hand, sanctioned unpaid maternity leaves. Ironically, historians Seth Koven and Sonya Michel have argued that these state-supported programs were more extensive and generous in "strong" states (i.e. with well developed bureaucracies and traditions of government intervention) where large networks of female reform associations were weakest, like France and Germany. In the United States, on the other hand, women's voluntary associations were quite active at the turn of the twentieth century, but attained little in the form of maternal welfare.

After the bloodletting of World War I, maternal welfare took on added importance in Europe, though this rarely resulted in major new programs. Instead, as with social insurance, legislators consolidated existing schemes with little alteration to basic assumptions and structures. In many states, the goal remained to convince women to stay home and have more children. Fascist Italy and Germany, for example, implemented maternalist measures to rebuild their populations, while forcing many women to leave better-paying jobs to be replaced by unemployed men. The major exception to this lack of innovation was Sweden, where, between 1933 and 1938, politicians implemented such programs as state-subsidized loans for newlyweds; maternity benefits for approximately 90 percent of all mothers, including free childbirth services; and low-interest housing loans for large families.

The Soviet Union represented the other great exception to this trend of consolidation without innovation during the interwar years. With the success of the Bolshevik revolution and subsequent civil war, the creation of the soviet state opened up a new era for Russia's poor. Within the span of approximately one decade, poor relief went from a very traditional arrangement of aid, with few state initiatives to supplement private charity and informal community networks, to one of the world's most advanced systems of social welfare. Soviet citizens enjoyed the constitutionally guaranteed right to employment and a whole range of services, all within a centralized, state-planned economy. Unlike the other nascent welfare states, however, the soviet system made the workplace, not the state itself, the chief purveyor of social services. Because the government expected every able-bodied person to work (with a short-lived program for unemployment benefits officially abolished in 1930), the state was able to subsidize factories and collective farms, which, in turn, provided housing, healthcare, childcare, leisure and cultural activities, and even vacation facilities for their employees. Unfortunately, through the workplace, the state also assumed a monopoly on furnishing these social services, for the existence of private charities would only imply that need and want persisted in the new workers' paradise. This proved disastrous when the system failed to meet collective and individual needs. As noted in the previous chapter, shortages in basic foodstuffs and housing kept living standards low throughout the Soviet Union in the 1920s and 1930s. In addition, employers, who were government functionaries, used social services, as well as government subsidies for basic consumer goods, to justify artificially low wages. Nevertheless, due to the ineffectiveness of poor relief in tsarist Russia, Soviet innovations were a real improvement on what they replaced.

In other regions of the world, the same solicitude that led to innovative schemes and increased state assistance in Europe, the United States and the Soviet Union did not always dramatically alter conventional solutions or strategies for coping with poverty. Change occurred in some places, but not enough to match the lead taken in Europe. The 1929 Relief and Protection

Law in Japan, for example, which politicians implemented only after intense public pressure in 1932, expanded the rolls of relief recipients by adding programs for medical care, childbirth, and occupational preparation (demonstrating a common concern with social reproduction), but eschewed social insurance for need-based aid for those unable to participate in the labor pool. In addition, local and regional government retained tremendous responsibility for funding relief, splitting the costs with the national government. One important innovation in this new legislation was the adoption of a minimum household budget for those on relief, a standard income that assistance had to preserve. Nevertheless, per capita standards of assistance in 1936 were only slightly higher than they had been in 1926. Meanwhile, in the British empire, growing unrest captured by the activities of the Indian National Congress on the subcontinent, and riots in the West Indies in 1937, spotlighted the continuing poverty in colonies that imperialists had promised to improve. Although this attention spurred on a series of public works campaigns to assist the able-bodied unemployed and culminated in the creation of a Social Services Division within the Colonial Office in 1939, efforts at more comprehensive reforms could not compete with the domestic concerns raised by the Depression and the coming world war. Until the next postwar period, then, state assistance throughout the colonies continued to emphasize famine relief and irregular public works schemes, with private charities left to fill the remaining gaps.

Elsewhere around the globe, a lack of funds, strong opposition to reform, or some combination of the two often stymied efforts to reform government poor relief. While Turkish reformers thus hoped to create an efficient system of social welfare as part of their general efforts at state-building and modernization in the 1920s and 1930s, traditionalists argued that individual duty and local community support had to remain the hallmarks of poor relief. Regardless, like many states in the uncertain years between the two world wars, Turkey had limited funds with which to construct the comprehensive system reformers advocated. In South Africa, on the other hand, although relief for poor whites increased in the 1930s, with state officials adopting the more standardized and comprehensive approach espoused by Western Europe and the United States, virtually all efforts to expand assistance to the larger population of poor blacks met with stiff resistance and disappeared completely with the 1948 electoral success of the National Party that instituted apartheid. So, while South Africans of European origins and a legally defined group of "Coloured" people benefited from a widening array of social services like old age pensions and aid to destitute mothers and children, all provided by the new Department of Social Welfare founded in 1933, impoverished and vulnerable black South Africans received almost nothing from the government. National officials limited state aid for poor blacks to food rations for the permanently destitute, short-term emergency relief for the conjunctural poor, and subsidies to a Bantu Refuge established in a former mining compound in 1927 as a home for the destitute. This did nothing for the rapidly growing number of able-bodied blacks impoverished by land alienation and low wages.

South African blacks also benefited little from the other great trend in poor relief, the establishment of large associations devoted to ameliorating conditions for the impoverished. Before 1945, most of these relief organizations limited themselves to working within national borders. Unfortunately, they also tended to thrive only in areas with a relatively free and well developed civil society and enough private wealth to support them. Such conditions were difficult to find in many parts of the world. Moreover, their success depended to a large extent on their ability to mirror popular views of poverty and charity. This, too, was not always easy. In Turkey, for instance, groups like the Red Crescent Society and the Children's Protection Society frequently found themselves embroiled in the sometimes bitter debate over expanded state assistance. They required official authorization, and often relied on friendly connections with government officials who sought to expand social welfare, but they also depended on contributions from those who continued to view charity as a private, intra-community matter. Similar problems arose in sub-Saharan Africa, where prevalent attitudes steadfastly supported indiscriminate charity meant to build patronage. Consequently, most aid institutions remained foreign-dominated, especially by Christian missionaries. Secular international relief agencies were slow to challenge that domination. The first of these, the Red Cross, founded in 1863, turned its attention to Africa only after World War I. The Save the Children Fund, established in 1919, devoted its energies at first to European children left destitute after the war, but, once conditions in Europe improved, sponsored an international conference on African children in Geneva in 1931. Unfortunately, the Depression and World War II intervened before much could be accomplished. So, as with so much that occurred in the realm of charity and poor relief during the interwar years, these efforts could only make silent promises to be kept after 1945.

In many regions of the world, then, despite significant transformations in the causes and nature of poverty, there was little change in institutional relief. In large parts of Asia, Latin America and sub-Saharan Africa, Christian missionaries retained a virtual monopoly on aid to the destitute, while feeble governments struggled to maintain the peace with emergency relief in times of widespread dire need. In Latin America and China, it was far more common during these years for public revenue to be spent on trying to preserve independence, either through defense modernization or state-sponsored industrialization. While the latter had the potential to ease poverty, such initiatives were too recent to have much impact before 1945. As a result, for many able-bodied poor, the primary means of support remained the extended family, community networks, and the informal economy. But here, too, change was evident during these years. In many instances, industrialization and imperialism made it difficult for families and communities to care for their own needy as indebtedness became more common. At the same time, the informal economy underwent significant alteration. Many poor, especially women, had survived by hawking common necessities like firewood, but more extensive transportation networks and the growth of the formal market began to undercut that traditional strategy. Fortunately, it also opened up new ones. Some of these hawkers became petty traders who specialized in minute quantities of common items, like needles, that other poor families could not afford to purchase in larger packages at local stores. In expanding urban areas, poor women fortunate enough to avoid prostitution also survived by offering services like sewing, hairdressing, and laundry. Just as common for many women in sub-Saharan Africa and Latin America was the expansion of the traditional female task of brewing, now centered on small unregulated taverns that punctuated the geography of growing slums. In an interesting combination of community networks and informal economics, some black female brewers in the slums of Johannesburg created self-help associations called *stokfels* that maximized their chances of survival. Members contributed a weekly sum to a shared pool. Once a week, one member used that fund to organize a neighborhood party where admission was charged. The hostess kept the proceeds, and the process started over again the following week. In the absence of the innovations that marked poor relief elsewhere, these women, like many others, followed the time-tested, though complicated and painful, strategy of patching together a makeshift economy. They survived, but their experiences fueled a growing sentiment that much more needed to be done for the world's poor.

Conclusion

Between 1880 and 1945, poor relief in much of the world underwent momentous changes, laying the groundwork for the welfare state and the growth of international relief agencies. As a result, while poverty became less life-threatening around the globe (so that famines and economic crises yielded far lower mortality rates than previously), relative poverty became the most prevalent form of impoverishment throughout most of the industrialized world. For the groups that traditionally comprised the destitute in particular – orphans, the elderly, and the infirm – social insurance and social welfare meant dramatic improvements in lifestyle. By 1933, for example, over 15.5 million widows, orphans, and elderly Britons were eligible for contributory social insurance pensions. Meanwhile, in Britain and other industrialized societies, even children in families, and not just the more limited group of orphans, benefited from school-related health clinics, infant care, and, in some places, municipally subsidized summer vacations to the countryside.

As important as they were for future developments, however, it would be a mistake to over-emphasize these transformations. First, in many parts of the world, like Latin America and sub-Saharan Africa, few benefited from these modifications in attitudes and options. Continuity marks the history of how the poor survived in these regions. Second, even where change occurred, limitations were evident. In the Soviet Union, for example, despite ground-breaking advances in recognizing the social and economic rights of ordinary citizens, the top-down system excluded the people from decision-making and bred alienation. Moreover, in the face of shortages and significant hardship, Soviet officials clung to an ideology that refused to acknowledge need in their midst. In the West, politicians did not design social welfare and social insurance to raise living standards, but only to prevent impoverishment. This was painfully clear during the Great Depression of the 1930s, when consumer demand plummeted and widespread unemployment ground economies to a virtual standstill. Third, where improvements did occur, they were typically restricted to urban areas, where new institutions and programs served concentrated and more obvious pockets of need and want. Rural poverty remained hidden and largely ignored.

More importantly, none of these changes altered some of the fundamental mechanisms that increased economic insecurity for certain groups during this period, especially women and disenfranchised racial groups. In industrialized societies, social insurance and social welfare were built on inequality, incorporating not only a class bias, but also a striking gender bias. For instance, most states adopted a male breadwinner approach to social insurance. One was not entitled to participate in insurance programs based on the rights of citizenship or even full-time employment, but because one was a male worker or part of his family. Single, full-time female workers received fewer benefits because the law assumed that they were not breadwinners for entire families, and married female workers received practically no benefits, as officials incorporated them into the system as wives, not workers. Furthermore, though maternalist social welfare helped many women, it did not allow them to integrate motherhood fully with their work lives. Many women found their options for paid employment narrowed once they became mothers. As a result, in many areas, as in less developed economies, community networks and the informal economy remained their best hope of survival. Fortunately, like the women who ran the *stokfels* in Johannesburg, these women proved determined and resourceful. Scholars continue to debate, therefore, whether or not maternalist benefits proved a boon or a drawback for women. To some, such policies continued to enclose women in a separate sphere that justified differential treatment while failing to recognize the full range of legitimate economic roles that women performed. For others, including some feminists, maternal social welfare fed aspirations that growing concern for motherhood would eventually lead to a revaluation of women's worth in society. As regards disenfranchised racial groups, however, such debates are mute. Either through unofficial pressures, as in the United States, or outright legal restrictions, as in South Africa, these groups remained largely outside many of the communities served by new welfare programs. Moreover, in most colonies, imperial masters rarely even considered implementing the policies and institutions that they were coming to accept as necessary in their own home countries. Again, neighborhood and kinship networks, as well as the limited opportunities afforded by the informal economy, were paramount in the survival of the poor in these disenfranchised populations. Despite the considerable transitions in poor relief before 1945, then, it is little wonder that proponents of reform readied themselves for even greater change as the Second World War drew to a close.

Further reading

On the origins of the welfare state: Peter Flora and Arnold J. Heidenheimer (eds) *The Development of Welfare States in Europe and America* (New Brunswick NJ: Rutgers University Press, 1981); Young-sun Hong, "Social Welfare and Insurance," *The Encyclopedia of European Social History* vol. 3 (New York: Charles Scribner's and Sons, 2001): 467–82; Seth Koven and Sonya Michel (eds) *Mothers of a New World: Maternalist Politics and the Origins of the Welfare State* (New York: Routledge, 1993). On developments in other industrialized states: Vic George and Nick Manning, *Socialism, Social Welfare, and the Soviet Union* (Boston MA: Routledge and Kegan Paul, 1980); W. Dean Kinzley, "Japan's Discovery of Poverty," *Journal of Asian Studies* 22, 1 (1988): 1–24; Koji Taira, "Public Assistance in Japan: Development and Trends," *Journal of Asian Studies* 27, 1 (1967): 95–109. On charity outside of Western Europe and the United States: Michael Bonner, Mine Ener and Amy Singer (eds) *Poverty and Charity in Middle Eastern Contexts* (Albany NY: SUNY Press, 2003); Mine Ener, *Managing Egypt's Poor and the Politics of Benevolence, 1800–1952* (Princeton NJ: Princeton University Press, 2003); John Iliffe, *The African Poor* (New York: Cambridge University Press, 1987); Adele Lindenmeyr, *Poverty is Not a Vice: Charity, Society, and the State in Imperial Russia* (Princeton NJ: Princeton University Press, 1996).

Chapter 6

Poverty and poor relief after 1945

In April 1945, as the wars in Europe and Asia drew to a close, delegates from around the globe gathered in San Francisco to lay the groundwork for a new international organization. During the previous eight years, over 48 million men, women, and children had died, intensive bombing had destroyed infrastructure throughout Asia and Europe, and desperate refugees had overrun cities of rubble. Even in many of the nations left relatively unscathed, the end of wartime economic restrictions and an eminent flood of demobilized veterans threatened rampant inflation and unemployment. Is it any wonder, therefore, that as the delegates conferred, economic issues and reconstruction remained close to the top of their agenda and figured prominently in the Charter they completed in June? Among its provisions, the Charter acknowledged in Article 55 that the "creation of conditions of stability and well-being . . . are necessary for peaceful and friendly relations among nations." To that end, the members of this new United Nations pledged to "promote higher standards of living, full employment, and conditions of economic and social progress and development."

This early step in the internationalization of poor relief, with its new focus on global cooperation for creating robust economic conditions, reflects the most significant trends in the history of world poverty after 1945: globalization and the growing importance of development. In this context, globalization refers to both the increasing connectivity of the world's populations and the interdependence of national markets, while development implies not just an increase in wealth, but also the restructuring of economies to sustain lasting prosperity. Together, these trends had three main impacts. First, very few people continued to accept poverty as part of the natural order. Instead, throughout the world, most came to see it as something that must be eradicated. Second, poverty's causes *and* solutions became inexorably tied to global forces. In addition to the intensification of global commerce, the postwar years witnessed the unprecedented creation of numerous and varied international agencies devoted solely to combating and preventing need and want far outside the regions where these institutions are headquartered. Finally, the bulk of these efforts focused primarily upon the problem of structural poverty, the misery that afflicts the able-bodied who cannot find paid employment, or whose wages are too low to support themselves and their families. Divided into sections on the nature and causes of impoverishment and economic insecurity, perceptions of poverty and its alleviation, and the strategies such attitudes engendered, this chapter examines the process by which globalization and development produced those results.

The nature and causes of poverty

To a great extent, the nature and causes of poverty in the decades after 1945 underwent few major alterations. Instead, earlier patterns expanded their impacts and intensified. In particular, the roots of economic insecurity for the vast majority of the world's population became inexorably tied to global forces, especially international trade, while the nature of hardship for many shifted from a lack of basic necessities, like food and shelter, to the inability to participate fully in normative patterns of consumption. At the same time, as state administrations developed in the wake of decolonization and superpower support during the Cold War, the power of public officials either to alleviate or inflict misery through taxation, bureaucratization, and armed conflict increased. Finally, the gap between poor and rich nations mushroomed, demonstrating that while globalization has generated great wealth, these riches were not distributed equally.

At the heart of many of these developments lies the world economy. Indeed, it is virtually impossible to understand the fluctuations in the numbers of people suffering from need and want after World War II without examining the dynamics of international trade. As subsistence agriculture all but disappeared after 1945 and industrialization spread to parts of Asia and Latin America, more people entered into a complex, global network of trade and production. Cotton from India, for example, was woven into garments in East Asia, which were then sold in North America and Europe. Automobiles assembled in the United States comprised parts manufactured in Asia and Latin America. Computers from Brazil furnished offices in sub-Saharan Africa, while call centers in India supported high-tech and service industries all over the English-speaking regions of the world. In fact, the ratio of exports to world GDP rose from 5.5 percent in 1950 to 17.2 percent in 1998. Moreover, these figures convey neither the large number of businesses that sustained the export market through local commerce, nor the importance of international finance to the overall health of many national economies. In this environment, economic insecurity often resulted from shifts in global commerce, particularly as first customs unions and then free trade agreements became more prominent in world trade. Textile workers in Europe and North America, for instance, lost their jobs as multinational corporations seeking lower labor costs opened new factories in Latin America and Asia. Similarly, the success of Japanese automobiles in international markets meant plant closures in the West. As with the Great Depression of the 1930s, in such an interconnected system of commerce, economic crises, like the oil shortages of 1973 and 1979, had tremendous impacts, sparking inflation and job loss in many different regions. As nations switched their currencies to a floating exchange system in the 1970s, shifts in capital markets had the same impacts. In the 1990s, the loss of foreign reserves resulted in economic crises in nations as different from one another as Thailand, Mexico, and India. Finally, in markets that still relied upon the production of raw materials like sugar, minerals, and coffee, still quite common in Latin America and sub-Saharan Africa, the patterns and risks associated with colonial and neocolonial trade continued to produce widespread poverty and economic insecurity.

The power of the state to influence people's livelihood was another enduring pattern in the history of world poverty after 1945, one that expanded its impact as public administrations developed more fully around the globe. This was a double-edged sword, however. As in earlier periods, the state could decrease vulnerability by promoting healthcare, education, and economic development, or it could inflict hardship through corruption, over-taxation, and the official sanction of exploitive labor patterns. In Latin America, for instance, a new generation of populist leaders in the 1930s and 1940s responded to the collapse of their export markets due to the Great Depression by supporting import-substitution industrialization (ISI). Designed to replace imported consumer items by building native industries, ISI typically entailed tremendous state expenditures and was often accompanied by generous labor contracts and the early outlines of a welfare state. Until the 1970s, then, government policies in these regions drove down national poverty rates and promoted the expansion of both the middle and working classes, although hardship continued to dog the peasants since these programs rarely included significant land redistribution in the countryside. Other states, however, adopted strategies that provoked extensive misery. In China, as earlier in the Soviet Union, the drive to industrialization incorporated the collectivization of agriculture. This sparked the deadliest famine in history. Approximately 30–40 million people perished during China's attempted "Great Leap Forward" between 1958 and 1960. Famine mortality also increased in sub-Saharan Africa after 1960. This was often due to civil wars or the breakdown of state administrations, which prevented aid from reaching those in need. This occurred in Nigeria during the Biafran War, when 1.5 million people died between 1967 and 1969, and in Somalia, where approximately 300,000 starved to death in the early 1990s because warring factions interrupted food deliveries. Finally, public officials sometimes ruined the economic health of their countries by borrowing extensively and saddling their populations with insurmountable debt. At times leaders adopted this policy with the best of intentions, as when Latin

American states like Brazil borrowed to finance development schemes as the benefits of ISI began to wane in the late 1960s, but in many other instances, corrupt leaders funneled international loans into private bank accounts while lending agencies turned a blind eye. Ferdinand Marcos of the Philippines, for example, grew rich because the United States needed his nation as a fundamental part of Cold War strategies. Money that should have gone to the alleviation and prevention of poverty instead supported a lavish lifestyle for an elite few.

Not all long-term trends were negative, however. For more and more of the world's population, for example, poverty became relative, not absolute. Much of this was due to the Green Revolution – the development of new hybrid strains of basic grains like wheat, rice and corn that dramatically improved yields. While the amount of land under cultivation in the world increased by only 1 percent between 1950 and 1992, yields of coarse grain grew approximately threefold. In Mexico, where scientists working under Norman Borlaug ushered in the first of these new strains, wheat yields doubled in approximately ten years, and allowed the country to shift from a net importer to a net exporter of wheat by 1964. India and Pakistan achieved similar results thanks to the new hybrid strains of grain combined with extensive chemical fertilization, expanded irrigation, pesticide use, and mechanization. India in particular transformed itself from a site of recurring famine to one of the world's largest food producers. Thanks to these innovations, many areas of Asia and Latin America achieved food security – i.e. the ability to grow enough food to feed the population – despite continued population growth. Although criticism from environmentalists was mounting by the century's end, and food insecurity continued to plague approximately 2 billion people around the world, especially in sub-Saharan Africa, the Green Revolution banished the specter of hunger in much of the world.

Relative poverty also became a more prevalent form of impoverishment as the world's wealth increased. Between 1950 and 1998, world GDP (gross domestic product) rose approximately sixfold, while real per capita income grew by 2.1 percent a year. In fact, some scholars refer to the period between 1950 and 1973 as the "golden age" of the capitalist era, with our current age, since 1973, as second-best. In part, globalization itself is responsible for this, for it generated increased affluence, and not just in the traditionally rich nations of Western Europe and North America. In Asia, export-driven industrialization in the four "little dragons" of South Korea, Taiwan, Singapore and Hong Kong raised income levels and fostered vibrant consumer markets. This extension of manufacturing, often operating in tandem with the spread of multinational corporations and the expansion of state bureaucracies, enlarged the ranks of the middle classes, as it did in Latin America. At the same time, industrialization was particularly benefi-cial to the poor in these Asian nations, since income distributions remained fairly egalitarian. During the 1990s in South Korea, for instance, the richest 20 percent of the population earned 5.2 times more than the poorest 20 percent. Unfortunately, elsewhere in the world, income distributions are much higher. In Brazil, the ratio is 25.5:1. Moreover, the gap between rich and poor nations only expanded as the world's wealth increased. In 1900, the ten richest countries in the world were nine times as rich as the ten poorest. Sixty years later, they were thirty times as rich. By 1999, they were sixty-five times as rich.

In this evolving context of change and continuity, poverty took many faces throughout the world. Among the destitute, for instance, children, the elderly, and the infirm still comprised the majority of those who could not survive without assistance, yet some of the underlying causes of their poverty changed. After the 1980s, HIV/AIDS, drug addiction, and mental illness became more prominent triggers of indigence and homelessness in both affluent and poor regions of the world. At the other end of the spectrum, conjunctural, or crisis, poverty, which afflicts those who ordinarily provide for themselves and their families, continued to follow in the wake of calamity. Such catastrophes arose from varied sources; from more traditional causes like the violence of open warfare and natural disasters, to the increasingly common crises of economic and state collapse. While the latter causes tended to strike relatively new states created during the decolonization period of the 1960s, and those weak economies reliant on the production of raw materials, economic downturns in the 1970s and the collapse of the Soviet Bloc in the 1990s demonstrated that in a global economy, few were immune to crisis. Ironically, as we will see later in this chapter, attempts to promote economic development, like the structural adjustment programs that swept through Latin America in the 1980s, could also swell the ranks of the conjunctural poor.

The greatest diversity in the causes and nature of poverty after 1945, as in previous centuries, existed among the structural poor. On the one hand, in mature industrial economies, particularly in Western Europe and the United States, well paying, secure jobs in the manufacturing sector became more difficult to find after the 1970s. For some, economic security re-emerged in a burgeoning information sector dependent upon advanced technology, but such positions typically required advanced education. In this new environment, then, poverty arose from a lack of education and a resulting reliance on jobs in the lower-paying service sector, which also expanded during these years. Because such employment, in tandem with an advanced social welfare system, limited the threat of hunger and homelessness to only a relatively small minority, poverty in these societies frequently took the form of social exclusion and extreme economic insecurity. In the United States, those who suffered from this type of poverty were often referred to as "the working poor". In some of these societies, race and gender could be ancillary causes of such misery, as institutional racism made it more difficult for minorities to find places in institutions of higher education and women struggled to balance employment with motherhood. Indeed, an increasing divorce rate, coupled with insufficient salaries from the service-sector jobs that required few qualifications, swelled the ranks of women and children among the poor in many Western nations. While workers in the new industrial powerhouses of Asia avoided such difficulties before the financial crisis of the 1990s, in the early years of the twenty-first century it was as yet unclear if recovery from such conjunctural poverty would entail an increase in large, long-standing pockets of structural poverty. The same was true of the former Soviet Bloc economies slowly making the difficult transition to free-market economics.

In the transitional economies of Latin America and parts of Asia, on the other hand, where fledgling industries co-existed with more traditional forms of manufacturing and agriculture, lack of employment opportunities remained the most significant cause of structural poverty, but this was nothing new. In these areas, widespread unemployment and underemployment dated back much farther than 1945, sparked by a process of land alienation that only intensified in the postwar global economy and the rise of agri-business. In addition, over-population exacerbated the problem, giving rise to hyper-urbanization and overcrowded shanty towns in the shadows of more prosperous housing districts. For many of the structural poor in these areas, the lack of adequate shelter, clean running water, and basic education and health services was a far more significant marker of indigence than social exclusion. In the 1980s, however, yet another dimension to impoverishment arose in some of these regions, especially Latin America. Structural adjustment policies forced many heavily indebted states to cut their budgets, leaving numerous middle-class managers and civil servants in the lurch, including those who had worked in state-subsidized industries. In places like Argentina, this "new poor" comprised families living in comfortable housing, headed by men and women who had attained high levels of education, but whose income had fallen below national poverty lines. In addition, they doggedly rejected any reference to themselves as "poor" and resisted any change in their bourgeois appearance. As with many of the impoverished in the former Soviet Bloc, it was still unclear at the start of the twenty-first century whether or not their indigence would prove a temporary aspect of economic transition, or a permanent aspect of the economic insecurity that accompanies liberal economics.

Finally, in those regions still dominated by agriculture, like sub-Saharan Africa, South Asia, and Southeast Asia, the trade imbalances and social conditions generated by an over-reliance on international markets for raw materials continued to yield the same high rates of structural poverty they had during the nineteenth century. In addition, as in transitional economies, overpopulation and land alienation have sparked hyper-urbanization and an increase in the number of people living in harsh, unsanitary conditions because these cities lack both infrastructure and available jobs. In India, the Green Revolution only intensified this process, as the cost of fertilizers and mechanization allowed wealthy farmers to buy out their smaller neighbors who could not afford to compete. The number of landless in rural areas of the subcontinent thus grew to 50 million in the 1990s, up from 27.9 million in 1951. Moreover, these statistics exclude the vast numbers who chose to immigrate to urban areas in search of jobs. In Greater Bombay/ Mumbai, for example, the population exploded from almost 3 million to 9.9 million during those same years. It is not surprising, therefore, that most of the approximately sixty-six countries that the World Bank characterized as having the lowest per capita national income in 2001 ($745 or less) can be found in these regions, which were also home to the lion's share of the world's 840 million undernourished people in 2002.

In the history of world poverty, then, continuity marks much of the focus on the causes and nature of impoverishment. Change was certainly evident, but it could not obscure the intensification and widening impacts of patterns established well before 1945. The same cannot be said of perceptions of indigence and its possible remedies, however, which underwent a significant sea change under the world's growing fixation on the concept of development.

Attitudes toward poverty and its alleviation

After 1945, the belief that poverty was a natural aspect of society disappeared, replaced by the widespread view that it could and should be abolished. The remarkable recovery of Western Europe and Japan, as well as the unprecedented prosperity of the 1950s and 1960s, only fueled such attitudes. In this atmosphere, the concept of development came to dominate the world of poor relief. For most, development was short-hand for industrialization. It rested on the idea that material conditions improved when labor productivity increased, usually via mechanization. Even in the midst of the Cold War, this was one principle that the West and the Soviets seemed to agree upon (despite China's disastrous attempt to steer its own course before the late 1970s). In rhetoric at least, both sets of adversaries often aimed to promote industrialization among their client states through a complex mix of grants, loans, and favorable trade agreements, while potential allies sought to play both sides off of each other in search of the best deal for achieving the basic necessities for mechanization. Egypt's Gamal Abdel Nasser, for example, turned from the United States to the Soviet Union in the aftermath of the 1956 Suez Crisis to achieve his desire for a high dam at Aswan. The dam would both enhance agricultural productivity, increasing the capital available for investment, and provide for the electrification of the countryside, another prerequisite of industrialization. If the desirability of economic development won general approval during these years, however, there was little agreement over two other related issues: the best path for achieving it, on the one hand, and the exact nature of the desired end-product, on the other. Conflict over these two concerns monopolized much of the debate over poverty and shaped divergent attitudes over the best means for alleviating poverty into the twenty-first century.

In the immediate decades following World War II, most scholars in the West adopted the view that industrialization occurred naturally as a fundamental aspect of "modernization." Although there was little consensus over what exactly triggered the shift away from agriculture and handicrafts, with potential causes ranging from cultural values and religion to climate and geography, many agreed that the Western model indicated a progressive process that followed various developmental stages. The policy implications of such views tended to emphasize reforms to produce some of the same conditions that accompanied industrialization in Western Europe, like the reorganization of education, the attempt to lower birth rates, and the implementation of legal guarantees for private property. This school presented no clear blueprint for success, however. In fact, even before 1945, the Soviet system had offered a significant variation on this approach by emphasizing the role of the state in achieving industrialization. By collectivizing agriculture and controlling the economy, public officials made the Soviet Union an industrial power and offered others a more deliberate, albeit painful, path to development. Unfortunately, as Mao's China demonstrated, following that path often proved easier to imagine than to realize. Moreover, the Soviet Union typically failed to provide as much support to client states as its rhetoric implied, preferring instead to retain such allies as useful suppliers of raw materials and ready markets for Soviet-made goods, much as the imperialist West did with its colonies and less developed allies.

In the 1970s, however, faith in modernization began to wane as a new group of scholars highlighted the difficulty that producers of raw materials experienced in gathering enough capital to engage in their own economic development. Because raw materials earned less on the international market than manufactured goods, these countries suffered from serious trade imbalances. Moreover, even the profits from raw materials rarely benefited the host populations, since the plantations and processing plants were often owned by foreign investors. In short, as we saw in Chapter 4, these nations were dependent on industrialized states, giving this school of thought its designation, "dependency theory." Left to the natural development of this economy, these states would never achieve industrialization and the increased labor productivity that would end poverty. Many dependency theorists thus proposed a new direction for development. To a certain extent, their policies justified actions that some Latin American leaders had implemented in the wake of the Great Depression, ISI. Import Substitution Industrialization, like Soviet socialism, emphasized the role of the state in promoting industrialization, but not to the extent of completely overturning the capitalist free market. Instead, politicians in places like Brazil and Argentina used state revenue to help bankroll semi-public industries designed to free their economies from the need to import goods from industrialized states. In addition, tariffs and price controls protected these businesses from foreign competition and enhanced their ability to reach a wider national market. Unfortunately, despite a few initially prosperous decades, these policies proved unsuccessful. In particular, without land reform and significant attempts to equalize income distribution, these new industries soon saturated their home markets but were not yet stable enough to compete internationally. In addition, many Western industries circumvented tariff restrictions by building plants in Latin America. While these provided some employment, they still drew the bulk of profits out of Latin America and back into the United States and Western Europe. Finally, because politicians frequently based ISI on populist politics, their regimes proved unstable in the long run, limiting the willingness of wealthy individuals and institutions from investing in further development and fostering strident dissent from traditional elites. In the end, some officials, including the military elites who had seized power in a number of Latin American countries in the 1970s, turned to foreign loans as a means of maintaining economic growth. When interest rates skyrocketed, the result was financial ruin.

In the midst of this distress, a new, neoclassical, perspective emerged in the 1980s and 1990s, particularly in the United States and Western Europe. According to this approach, the key to successful development, and increased labor productivity, was investment in both human and physical capital. But, as the Latin American experience made evident, poor states found it almost impossible to sustain the large capital expenditures required for this. Only private investment could provide the necessary funds. In what became known as the "Washington Consensus," scholars and officials affiliated with aid agencies like the World Bank and the International Monetary Fund thus argued that the state's principal role in fostering economic development was to adopt policies that encouraged private investment. These "Structural Adjustment Programs" encouraged the exact opposite of what leaders had implemented during ISI, emphasizing "fiscal discipline," or the dramatic reduction of state spending in order to balance budgets and stabilize currencies, and "trade liberalization," or the reduction of tariffs, the abolition of price controls, and the establishment of more realistic exchange rates. Supporters often cited Uganda as an example of successful economic growth as a result of structural adjustment. After suffering economic ruin under the brutal dictatorship of Idi Amin, the nation and its people foundered under immense debt in the 1970s and 1980s. With the implementation of structural adjustment programs, however, the economy began to grow in the 1990s, averaging growth rates of 7 percent annually thanks to a revived and diversified agricultural sector. Critics argued, however, that the industrial sector continued to lag behind, still accounting for only 6 percent of the GDP in the 1990s. In other words, the nation's economy was merely reviving its dependent status and benefiting from a general improvement in international trade, not economic development. More importantly, the wealth generated by such growth only exacerbated social inequality and did little to alleviate mass poverty. Indeed, "fiscal discipline" frequently produced the groups of "new poor" discussed above.

As this debate over the best path to development raged on, scholars also raised the second major issue that marked concern with global poverty after 1945, the ultimate goal of economic growth. Traditionalists argued from the Western, liberal example that as industrial society matured, it ensured a gradual amelioration of social inequality and poverty by generating increased wealth. Building on a socialist legacy, however, many rejected this view in favor of a greater emphasis on egalitarianism. They argued instead that development had to be tailored to suit the needs of social justice. In Cuba, for example, Fidel Castro's regime emphasized education and health-care over private property and individual investment, despite convincing data that the latter was more apt to induce rapid industrialization and economic growth. Such arguments attracted broad support in a number of impoverished nations throughout Latin America and sub-Saharan Africa, particularly with aid from the Soviet Union, but receded in importance after the fall of the Soviet Union in 1991 (though not in Cuba). Of course, the prominence of equality and justice did not have to rest on a socialist foundation. During the 1960s, in the midst of a wide-ranging revival within the Catholic church, a group of Latin American theologians began to lay the groundwork for a movement known as Liberation Theology. These prelates placed far more weight on raising standards of living through a more equitable distribution of wealth than on economic development via industrialization. They interpreted the Bible to highlight not only aid to the poor, but also Old Testament practices that fostered equality of conditions. In the 1980s, however, the movement receded after persecution from secular leaders in Latin America and papal pressure to conform to the Vatican's more traditional teachings.

Ironically, at the same time, in some Western nations that had already begun to implement welfare programs before 1945 and, as we will see below, reinforced these systems during the 1950s and 1960s, a more unsympathetic stance toward social welfare also arose during the 1980s. In academic circles, for instance, some scholars argued that the true impact of various state programs was social control. Not only did government assistance sanction and promote the middle-class values that drove the commercial economy, but welfare measures also gave public officials new tools for policing the actions of aid recipients. Social workers became the shock troops who defined and monitored "proper" relationships, activities and attitudes. While these views had little impact outside of colleges and universities, on the other end of the political spectrum, the revival of neoclassical economics provoked far more extensive consequences. To a certain extent, these conservative criticisms sprang from the economic difficulties of the 1970s and the growing fear that these aging industrial states could not afford to maintain their increasingly over-burdened social programs. More often than not, however, opponents expressed these concerns in moral terms. They cursed the welfare state for promoting a culture of entitlement. Under the leadership of Ronald Reagan in the United States and Margaret Thatcher in the United Kingdom, for example, conservatives argued that too many Americans and Britons had lost any sense of individual responsibility, insinuating also that more economic difficulties awaited populations that no longer fostered personal initiative and self-reliance. In addition, they claimed that fraud ran rampant in the system, reminiscent of older arguments concerning the "undeserving poor." At times, such assertions were tinged with racism, implying that welfare was a way of life for minorities. In Europe, fringe politicians even earned greater popular appeal by arguing that many recipients did not truly belong to the nation, since they were recent immigrants. Arguing that the state had therefore to reduce its interference in economic matters, these leaders and their successors oversaw a spate of welfare reforms and privatizations that often reduced social services, sometimes in the name of strengthening the moral fabric of the nation.

As this brief discussion of welfare reform demonstrates, debates over poverty and development had significant policy ramifications. For better or worse, arguments over the best means of promoting economic sustainability and the desired end-product of economic growth generated a wide range of concrete actions after 1945. Some of these followed predictable patterns, such as the continued creation of state programs to promote social welfare. Others, however, veered off in new directions, spurred in large part by both the growing sense that the problem of poverty could be solved, and the emerging faith in international efforts at poor relief and development. These are the prime subjects of this chapter's next section.

Social welfare, poor relief, and development

While the causes of poverty after 1945 underwent few major changes, and attitudes toward its alleviation simultaneously witnessed significant transformations, the strategies for fighting impoverishment during these years experienced a more balanced mixture of both continuity and change. Among the poor themselves, for example, reliance on networks of family and friends, formal and informal employment, and assistance from state and private agencies all continued to make up the bulk of their economy of makeshifts. At the same time, the growth of public social welfare programs, like old age pensions, healthcare, and unemployment insurance, resumed after the interruption of the Great Depression and World War II. Though far from alone,

Britain signaled the clearest willingness to revive prewar social spending when it commissioned the famed Beveridge Report in 1942. In fact, thanks to the exceptional prosperity of the immediate postwar decades and the widespread acceptance of Keynesian economics, which promoted public spending as a means of maintaining economic health, politicians throughout Europe devised a new rationale and purpose for social welfare. Whereas late nineteenth-century and interwar programs aimed chiefly to prevent misery among those who were most susceptible to impoverishment, postwar social welfare assumed the new responsibility of raising standards of living for society as a whole. In addition to more generous means-tested assistance for the indigent, tax-supported universal coverage for healthcare, childcare, old age pensions, and education were meant to free up incomes for greater consumer spending. In some nations, like Sweden, maternalist welfare also strove to assume virtually all the costs for social reproduction, freeing mothers to participate as fully as they chose in the formal economy. In all, the goal was no longer the alleviation of material insufficiency, but the elimination of social exclusion. Meanwhile, outside of Europe, social welfare developed a strong connection to modernization, prompting even non-industrialized states to increase public expenditures although their budgets could scarcely cope with the added burden. Welfare programs became common features of nation-building from Latin America to East Asia, from sub-Saharan Africa to the Middle East.

As for changes to existing poverty reduction strategies, the most significant alterations involved the new focus on development, via a host of loans and grants, and the internationalization of aid. In part, this built on precedents set just before the war, when some European colonial powers, like Britain, established infant social welfare departments in their colonial offices. When the war ended, these states hoped to reaffirm their imperial presence by touting "community development" as a prime rationale for colonialism. After 1945, this movement expanded under the umbrella of international cooperation established by the United Nations, which gave rise to a host of institutions and programs designed to study global problems like poverty and to alleviate the most conspicuous examples of need and want. The Cold War cemented this new approach by sparking a competition for allies throughout the world. The United States in particular sought to use financial support as a means of promoting stability in states that encircled the Communist Bloc. Finally, the shining example of European recovery after implementation of the Marshall Plan strengthened faith in development assistance as a sound policy for raising living standards around the world. This all set the stage for the international organizations, both public and private, that became a mainstay of poor relief during the latter half of the twentieth century.

The transformation of a very traditional form of assistance, the charitable association, was a perfect indication of these changes. After 1945, these relief agencies, representing a sizeable portion of the burgeoning field of non-government organizations, or NGOs, began to separate into roughly two categories: mutual benefit associations and public benefit organizations. The first tended to focus their programs on local communities and participating members, and thus reflected the growth of development issues more prominently than internationalization. Perhaps the most famous example of these wide ranging associations was the Grameen Bank, launched in 1976 in Bangladesh by the economist Mohammad Yunnus. The Grameen Bank specialized in microcredit, offering small low-interest loans to the rural poor so that they could establish their own businesses or purchase equipment that would make their existing endeavors more profitable. Targeting the landless poor with no collateral for traditional loans, the Grameen Bank used small-group dynamics and collective responsibility to ensure repayment; capital became more readily available for all based on the repayment record of initial loan beneficiaries. In addition, because the ultimate goal was the alleviation of poverty, Grameen officials formed their small groups primarily among women, arguing that their success had a greater impact on the vitality of individual households. Moreover, after a group attained a clear record of reliability, capital for community improvement, like sanitation infrastructure and housing, became more available, which bank officials also encouraged the group to monitor for the entire community. Finally, group meetings encouraged these women to take a greater interest in wider political and social issues, making them active participants in the civic life of their villages and regions. In the 1980s, the Grameen Bank's success sparked the spread of microcredit institutions in other parts of the world, leading to the creation of the Foundation for International Community Assistance (FINCA), which espoused village banking. This placed greater control of credit into the hands of the poor themselves, but otherwise remained true to many of the original ideals of the Grameen Bank, with loans remaining relatively small, from $50 to $1,000. By 2002, FINCA's network of village banks had spread to twenty different countries, disbursing loans totaling $136 million to over a quarter of a million participants.

While such mutual benefit associations had their roots in earlier forms of self-help, like European "friendly societies" and the *stokfels* of South Africa's slums (though these had little to do with economic development), public service NGOs traced their ancestry back to more traditional charities, albeit with a stronger interest in economics and a much more pronounced international scope. According to some scholars, this was a natural progression for charities, as they moved from assistance, to small-scale self-reliance projects, to, eventually, a "third generation strategy" of "sustainable systems development." Unlike their mutual benefit cousins, these organizations tended to be headquartered in developed nations. They split their efforts between raising funds and awareness in affluent regions, on the one hand, and sponsoring and monitoring assistance programs, on the other. One of the most celebrated of these associations is Oxfam, originally the Oxford Committee for Famine Relief, founded in 1942 to provide assistance for refugees in Greece and then Europe as a whole. As conditions improved, however, Oxfam shifted its attention to developing countries in the 1960s. In addition to customary concerns with emergency relief in cases of widespread conjunctural poverty, the organization also began to promote sustainability in poor rural communities. In particular, they helped farmers learn the skills and acquire the resources to compete effectively in regional and international markets. So successful were NGOs like Oxfam, that during the 1980s and 1990s public international relief agencies and even some governments began to filter more and more of their funds through these private organizations. Most scholars agree, however, that NGOs would never have sufficient resources to produce the large-scale transformations necessary to ending poverty for the approximately 2.8 billion people who lived on $2 a day or less in 2000. That would require far more concerted international attention from public officials.

This more focused attention on the part of the world's leaders represented the clearest evidence of the new concern with development and internationalization. Much of this activity, and the various public agencies it spawned, came under the nominal oversight of the United Nations and its Economic and Social Council (ECOSOC). These organizations were multilateral – made up of individual member states – and, like NGOs, they divided into two main categories. The first includes those that are organized according to a dollar-a-vote principle. In other words, decision-making within these bodies is weighted to favor those who provide the most funding for their operations, not the recipients of their grants and loans. The most prominent examples of these agencies are the World Bank and the International Monetary Fund (IMF), both of which emerged from the Bretton Woods Conference of 1944. The creators of the World Bank, which is comprised of the International Bank for Reconstruction and Development (IBRD), the International Development Association (IDA), the International Finance Corporation (IFC), the Multilateral Investment Guarantee Agency (MIGC), and the International Centre for Settlement of Investment Disputes (ICSID), originally intended it to help finance the recovery of Europe after the war. It pooled the money of its member states and used it to provide low-cost loans for applicants; the first, France, received $250 million in 1947. In the 1960s, however, as Europe's recovery neared completion, the World Bank began to focus more attention on developing countries. While the IBRD retained a range of fiscal requirements for loans that kept the poorest countries from attaining eligibility because they lacked creditworthiness, the IDA, founded in 1960, concentrated on long-term no-interest loans to nations that lacked such qualifications and where per capita GDP remained among the world's lowest. Until the 1970s, much of this assistance went toward the completion of specific projects, but, under the leadership of

Robert McNamara, the World Bank responded to criticism that isolated projects failed to spur on development and alleviate poverty without wider economic and social change. Therefore, both the IBRD and the IDA shifted to program funding with the conscious goal of reducing poverty through grants and long-term no- or low-interest loans. In the process, they dramatically increased the amount they allocated for development, up to $3 billion during the fiscal year 1972, more than three times what they had loaned out in 1968.

The World Bank altered its strategies once again in the 1980s when it began to work more closely with the IMF, adopting its neoclassical philosophy and expanding the conditionality of assistance. Unlike the World Bank, the IMF was never intended to be a development agency. Instead, its founding goal in 1944 was to stabilize the world currency market in order to facilitate world trade and prevent a reoccurrence of the financial crises that had plagued the interwar period. Circumstances forced it to change its policies in the 1970s, however, when many nations attached their currencies to a floating exchange rate and, in the wake of the global trade crisis, a number of debtor nations, especially in Latin America, threatened to default on their rapidly escalating international debt. So, in order to avert a more significant crisis, the IMF began to use the funds it acquired from its member-states to float loans to countries with payment difficulties. In cooperation with the World Bank, it also imposed neoclassical ideals and tied its assistance to structural adjustment plans (SAPs) aimed to correct any underlying problems that could lead to default. These could be so draconian that they were often described as "shock treatment" and, in the short term at least, they frequently exacerbated poverty. In response to the subsequent criticism, both organizations implemented the Heavily Indebted Poor Country (HIPC) Initiative in 1996, which targeted the world's poorest nations for more favorable debt relief. In addition, in 1999 they established a new requirement for assistance, Poverty Reduction Strategy Plans on the part of loan recipients. Linking the alleviation of poverty and a sense of direct participation to IMF and World Bank loans, these proposals included concrete steps drawn up by both borrower governments and the NGOs operating within the indebted country in order to protect the poor during structural adjustment and promote the growth of civil society. Nevertheless, criticism continued to mount. In particular, opponents decried the fact that two such powerful organizations made their most important decisions behind closed doors, where public scrutiny and debate held little sway.

The second group of multilateral agencies escaped much of this criticism because they were organized democratically, with all participants having an equal share in decision-making. Moreover, most of them operated more fully under the umbrella of the United Nations, with increased inspection from both the General Assembly and the international press. At the same time, however, they also had to balance concern for development with immediate demands for direct assistance in ways that the IMF and the World Bank did not. As a result, many of these agencies, like the World Health Organization, the World Food Program, the United Nations Children's Fund (UNICEF), and the Food and Agriculture Organization, spent a considerable portion of their resources on providing healthcare and maintaining food security where disease and malnutrition were most threatening. The United Nations Development Programme (UNDP) was a notable exception to this. Founded in 1965, three years after the UN declared its first Development Decade, the UNDP represented a shift away from the UN's early emphasis on gathering data and providing advice to members states to direct involvement. The UNDP provided grants for "sustainable human development," which included education, improved sanitation, and healthcare. Dependent upon the voluntary contributions of UN member states, the UNDP was particularly active in the field of urban poverty, spearheading the creation of the Urban Management Program, which strengthened the contribution of cities and towns to overall development in various nations, and the World Alliance of Cities against Poverty, which provided a clearinghouse of urban strategies for poor relief. Finally, the UNDP published the annual *Human Development Report*, a significant resource for understanding world poverty today.

Ironically, one of the most important multilateral agencies to surface after 1945 provided no monetary assistance at all; this was the Organization for Economic Cooperation and Development (OECD). Like many of the other multilateral organizations, its earliest incarnation arose from the ashes of World War II to coordinate European economic recovery and to oversee the use of funds from the Marshall Plan. By the end of the twentieth century, however, it grouped thirty developed nations together, including the United States and Japan, primarily to pool efforts at data collection and analysis on issues surrounding global poverty and economics. While as a whole the OECD adopted the role primarily of information clearinghouse and oversight, the twenty-one richest members formed the Development Assistance Committee (DAC) in 1960 to monitor and coordinate their strategies, both multilateral and bilateral, for promoting economic growth in the developing world. The DAC became the principal authority on development assistance, though it represented only those who provided such funds. It instituted a Common Aid Effort in 1961, but it enjoyed little power to enforce agreements or to ensure that goals were met. Instead, its primary tasks were to set such goals and to harmonize diverse policies by establishing norms for economic development. For instance, it defined true assistance, or Official Development Assistance (ODA), in 1972 as

> flows to developing countries and multilateral institutions provided by official agencies, including state and local governments, or by their executive agencies, each transaction of which meets the following test:

a) it is administered with the promotion of the economic development and welfare of developing countries as its main objective, and b) it is concessional in character and contains a grant element of at least 25 per cent.

In other words, in order to be considered ODA, instead of OOF (or Other Official Flows), assistance money must include a portion (at least 25 percent) that is in grant form, not a loan. At the same time, the DAC also set an overall goal of an 84 percent grant element for each individual member's ODA programs. Over the course of the twentieth century, the DAC also responded to criticisms of development programs by lobbying for greater consideration of "Basic Human Needs," and not just economic growth, in the later 1970s; better means of evaluating the effectiveness of aid in the 1980s; and good governance and environmental wellbeing in recipient nations in the 1990s. It was by those terms that both multilateral and bilateral development assistance was measured during those years.

Besides NGOs and multilateral agencies, bilateral agreements became another rich source of development assistance after 1945. Indeed, in 1996, almost 70 percent of all ODA from DAC members came in the form of direct aid from one nation to another. Despite this prominent role, bilateral assistance garnered the most criticism of all types of aid. This was due primarily to the conditions under which it was typically offered. Some countries, including the US and the UK, used ODA to subsidize indirectly their own arms industries, linking it to military debt cancellations. Others tied it directly to the purchase of goods from the donor country. In all, over a quarter of all ODA in 2000 (26.5 percent) was wholly contingent on purchases from DAC members. Moreover, some states made bilateral assistance a significant part of their foreign policy. Many European states, for example, used it to bind former colonies to the motherland, while the US subsidized governments it considered strategically important, both before and after the Cold War. By the end of the twentieth century, up to one third of all US ODA went to Israel and Egypt. It was this conditionality, and the thinly veiled political subtext of such aid, that raised the ire of many development specialists. In particular, they argued that bilateral aid lent itself more readily to corruption among donors and benefactors alike. Others argued, however, that the conditionality of such ODA allowed donors to use their expertise to target specific areas for development. In 2000, Japan allocated over 46 percent of its ODA to support transportation and industrial infrastructure. Unfortunately, past experiences also revealed many a dictator who lived extravagantly, like Haiti's Jean-Claude Duvalier, the Philippines' Ferdinand Marcos, and Zaire's Mobutu Sese Seko, thanks to pilfered ODA safely tucked away in secret bank accounts while their people suffered.

To address these concerns, as well as similar complaints about aid from the World Bank and IMF, DAC-member Norway proposed that the majority of ODA be filtered through the United Nations, where individual countries participate on a more equal basis and share collective responsibility for deciding which values to promote through international assistance. Perhaps nothing reflects just how much poor relief has changed since 1945 than this proposal and the responses to it. Not only had international aid become a given by the end of the century, but a full and varied network of agencies also existed to allocate that assistance. Moreover, funds to support development had become so central to diplomacy and international relations, that few nations greeted Norway's proposal with much enthusiasm. So, much as it had before the rise of the world economy, poor relief remained as important to the donor as it was to the benefactor.

Conclusion: reasons for optimism?

By the dawn of the twenty-first century, the internationalization of poor relief and the new goal of economic development gave many a reason to hope for a better future. In 1999, 23 percent of the world's population lived in extreme poverty, defined as earning less than $1 a day – a decrease from 30 percent nine years earlier. Furthermore, relative poverty had become the most prevalent form of impoverishment, as food security increased. Malnourishment affected 37 percent of the populations of developing nations between 1969 and 1971, but only 21 percent between 1990 and 1992. Moreover, thanks to an increased ability to muster global support for disaster relief, famine mortality rarely reached the levels it had before 1945. Another marker of poverty, infant mortality, also fell between 1970 and 2000, from 96 to 56 per 1,000 live births. In real terms, the total amount of ODA in 1994 was $56.7 billion (in 1993 prices). While that represented a downturn from the 1992 high of $59.6 billion, figures in 2002 revealed that DAC members were slowly reversing that trend. Donor countries increased their ODA by almost 5 percent from the previous year, raising it from 0.22 percent of GNP to 0.23 percent. This rise included a 12 percent increase in US aid, to $12.9 billion, and a 3 percent increase in EU aid, to $29.1 billion. Finally, as a clear indication of growing concern, the United Nations' General Assembly adopted a set of Millennium Development Goals in 2000 that included halving the proportion of people who live in extreme poverty and the proportion of people in hunger between 1990 and 2015. Thanks in large part to a dynamic economy, China, traditionally a home to many of the world's poor, had already reached that goal by 2003.

At the same time, there was still cause for great concern. In 2002, 840 million people still experienced malnutrition, a figure that exceeded the combined population of forty-two European countries. Hidden within this aggregate figure is the continued predominance of women, children, and the elderly among the world's poor, many dealing with very limited prospects for improving their circumstances. As the gulf between wealthy and poor nations widened almost annually, race too remained a significant marker of poverty throughout the world, though the success of Asian economies makes it increasingly difficult to portray this as a simple dichotomy between whites and everyone else. Compounding this situation, in sub-Saharan Africa, HIV/AIDS threatened to reverse positive trends in human development, like increased life expectancy. In Kenya, for example, life expectancy dropped by seventeen years, while Botswana witnessed a thirty-four-year decrease. Moreover, the former Communist Bloc became one more area of concern in the 1990s, in addition to the developing nations that the DAC traditionally targeted for ODA. Yet in the face of all of this, total ODA remained quite small, especially as a portion of the DAC member states' individual GNPs. Only five nations met the UN goal of 0.7 percent of GNP in 2003. And, while estimates indicated that an increase of at least $50 billion in additional aid was necessary to meeting the Millennium Development Goals, only $16 billion had been committed by 2003. As a result, many of the world's poor continue to rely primarily on social networks and an informal economy for survival, especially since significant portions of the women, children, and elderly who fall into this category enjoy very limited opportunities in the formal economy. Indeed, in the wake of hyper-urbanization, the informal economy has re-emerged as an important feature of the economy of makeshifts that still characterizes life for millions around the globe. So, as a new century opened, many could take solace in what had been accomplished since 1945. But, because the world had decided that poverty could be eradicated through sustainable economic development, all recognized that much remained to be done.

Further reading

Tim Allen and Alan Thomas, *Poverty and Development in the 21st Century* (New York: Oxford University Press, 2000); Alison Evans, *Poverty Reduction in the 1990s* (Washington DC: World Bank, 2000); Helmut Fuhrer, *A History of the Development Assistance Committee and the Development Cooperation Directorate in Dates, Names, and Figures* (Paris: OECD, 1996); Geoffrey Gilbert, *World Poverty* (Santa Barbara CA: ABC-Clio, 2004); and David C. Korten, *Getting to the 21st Century: Voluntary Action and the Global Agenda* (West Hartford CT: Kumarian Press, 1990). In addition, see the reports, publications, and websites of the world's major relief and development organizations, like the UNDP (including the annual *Human Development Report*), the World Bank (including the annual *World Development Report*), the IMF, the OECD, the Reality of Aid, and Oxfam.

Conclusion

This book opened with a brief discussion of poverty and its impacts in the East African nation of Mozambique. It is fitting, therefore, that we return there to conclude it. Before Portuguese colonization, Mozambique, though plagued by periodic droughts in the hinterland and torrential rains in the south, had become a rich source of gold and ivory for Islamic traders in the Swahili city-states along the coast and the independent Mwanamutapa kingdom inland. The Portuguese destroyed this exchange in the seventeenth century, and replaced it with a more extensive trade in slaves. Enslaved Mozambicans worked the plantations of Brazil and the Mascarene Islands in the Indian Ocean, as well as the new, largely independent *prazos*, or Portuguese plantations created in Mozambique itself. By the time of the late-nineteenth-century "Scramble for Africa," direct control of much of the colony had fallen to private companies in British hands, which oversaw construction of railway lines to link Mozambique to the English colonies of Southern Africa. Though the slave trade had ended by then, many Mozambicans now found themselves working as forced labor in British mines and plantations far from their homes. Little thought or effort went into Mozambique, however. By the time Portugal ceded its control in 1975, the new nation was among the poorest in the world. Unfortunately, independence brought no improvement, for it was accompanied by the widespread emigration of the white population and its capital, continued dependence on South Africa's more developed economy and a resulting trade imbalance, severe drought, and a prolonged civil war (fueled in part by Cold War manipulations) that lasted until 1992. The rapid spread of HIV/AIDS only exacerbated this misery in a nation where per capita GDP in the mid-1980s languished at only $120, and the government, which had mismanaged the economy for years, staggered under a virtually insurmountable international debt. But conditions improved toward the end of the twentieth century. Mozambique became the first nation to receive debt relief under the Heavily Indebted Poor Country (HIPC) Initiative launched by the World Bank and the IMF. By 2001, much of its debt had been either forgiven or restructured to make it more manageable. In addition, Mozambique received over $632

million in aid that year. Four years later, per capita GDP had risen to an estimated $1,300. While some of that increase came from high mortality due to
HIV/AIDS, it also reflected a GDP growth rate of 7 percent. As peace and
political stability returned, Mozambique became one of sub-Saharan Africa's
few success stories at the dawn of the twenty-first century.

This brief overview of poverty in Mozambique exhibits many of this
book's main themes. Throughout its history, the actual causes of impoverishment in Mozambique, as with the rest of the world, changed little. Drought
and other natural disasters resulted in crop failure, population growth put
pressure on limited resources, illness and disability wreaked havoc with individuals' abilities to care for themselves and their families, and warfare
disrupted trade and destroyed assets. At the same time, unequal systems of
resource distribution continually curbed people's capacity to cope with all of
this. What changed over time, however, was their vulnerability to these
sources of poverty. And Mozambique's history demonstrates that fluctuations
in that vulnerability became increasingly tied to the operation and impacts
of the world economy as it emerged and intensified after 1450. This began
with Portuguese colonization, which disrupted traditional trade routes,
expropriated resources, and extended the devastating impacts of slavery.
Moreover, instead of building an infrastructure that might have alleviated
traditional causes of poverty in this habitually drought-ridden part of Africa,
Portugal merely established new economic relationships that further impoverished much of the population. As with many other parts of the world,
imperialism in the industrial age only intensified these earlier patterns.
Mozambique specialized in low-value commodities like aluminum, prawns,
cashews, and cotton, while relying on import markets for more expensive
manufactured goods. After independence, a new socialist government sought
to reverse these impoverishing trends by harnessing the power of the state
for economic development, but mismanagement and the overwhelming scale
of the task before them only exacerbated the problem. This, too, reflected a
growing willingness among many nations to use the state to lessen poverty, a
condition that, in the popular mind, now required a solution and not just a
palliative. Finally, in the late twentieth century, Mozambique, like many
other developing nations, benefited from the internationalization of poor
relief, which began to focus on sustainable economic development.

How does all of this relate to world history as a whole? How does a better
understanding of poverty and the various strategies devised for its relief
promote a deeper understanding of world history? There are many possible
directions to take with those questions, but perhaps the most fruitful relates
poverty and poor relief to the nature of Western hegemony in the world.
This is a familiar narrative, one that has Western Europe growing in influence, wealth, and control up to the middle of the twentieth century.
Between roughly 1450 and 1750, these Atlantic powers managed to control
directly only Latin America and various coastal outposts in Asia and Africa.

While many historians now argue that China's thirst for silver was a far more prominent driving force in the rise of global commerce, the West still grew wealthy from this trade as the world's leading purveyor of merchant vessels. Enough so that it increased its influence in India and the Middle East; enough so that its own society became more complex and innovative. This helped drive the process of industrialization, which itself greatly enhanced the West's direct and indirect control over the rest of the globe while it expanded its own membership to include parts of Central Europe and the United States. Only Japan and Russia challenged that power by themselves beginning to industrialize. In the wake of the Great Depression and two world wars, however, the West's supremacy weakened. It gave way at first to bipolarity amidst decolonization, and then to what some scholars labeled geopolitical multipolarity. By the beginning of the twenty-first century, the West competed openly with industrializing powers in a resurgent East Asia, while internationalism seemed to dispute its prior claim to world leadership.

To a certain extent, of course, the history of world poverty confirms this interpretation, while adding some important nuances. It does this by reminding us that influence and hegemony may be much more subtle and indirect than outright control. Indeed, for much of the world's history since 1450, the West's influence rested primarily in economics. The colonization of Latin America, for example, spread hardship and misery to areas of sub-Saharan Africa where no European set foot until the nineteenth century. After industrialization, the West's economic power decimated traditional manufacturing in India and the Middle East alike, even though only the former experienced direct European rule. Ironically, at the same time, industrial poverty spread to Japan and Russia because they recognized the need to emulate the West in order to remain independent from it. What the history of poverty thus demonstrates is that the West's influence was often pervasive yet indirect. The West could have such wide ranging sway because its power lay in the operation of the world economy. Paradoxically, however, that fact also turns the traditional interpretation of world history on its head, emphasizing the West's continued dominance well beyond 1945. In essence, as some scholars argue, the ascendancy of "development" as an ideal for the entire world represents a victory for Western hegemony in cultural if not economic terms. Just as new welfare states deployed an army of social workers to help, but also impose norms on, the poor recipients of assistance, so development agencies raised experts to powerful positions as the arbiters of what developing nations should and should not do. And, as development scholar Arturo Escobar asserts:

> Instead of seeing change as a process rooted in the interpretation of each society's history and cultural tradition – as a number of intellectuals in various parts of the Third World had attempted to do in the 1920s and

1930s (Gandhi being the best known of them) – these professionals sought to devise mechanisms and procedures to make societies fit a pre-existing model that embodied the structures and functions of modernity [as the West defined it].

In short, then, with ODA and the power to shape the debate on how poverty should be eliminated, the West has maintained its influence well after decolonization limited its direct control around the globe.

But the history of world poverty can do much more than simply help us to understand more fully the contours of world history and the nature of Western hegemony. It reminds us of people's resilience in the face of both poverty and various efforts to mold their actions and thoughts. The informal economy and complex networks of family, neighbors, and friends have long served the poor and vulnerable as their first strategy when hard times strike, one that defies easy efforts at outside manipulation. In addition, the rise of the Grameen Bank and the wider global network of village banking, where the poor control the flow of assistance and target it to fit needs that they themselves define, reflects a growing awareness of the need to include aid recipients in the planning and implementation of any policies for sustainable economic development. Perhaps most importantly, however, history can serve as a call to action. An appreciation of who we are and where we have been prompts us to determine for ourselves what role we want to play in the world. Incorporating a better comprehension of poverty's history hopefully informs that determination. It reinforces the fact that in an age of increasing globalization, our actions have ramifications far beyond our circle of family and friends, our towns, and even our nations.

Further reading

Arturo Escobar, *Encountering Development: The Making and Unmaking of the Third World* (Princeton NJ: Princeton University Press, 1995); Jim Yong Kim, Joyce V. Millen, Alec Irwin and John Gershman (eds) *Dying for Growth: Global Inequality and the Health of the Poor* (Monroe ME: Common Courage Press, 2000); and Peter Townsend and David Gordon (eds) *World Poverty: New Policies to Defeat an Old Enemy* (Bristol: The Policy Press, 2002).

Notes

Introduction

1 The saying "money is the root of all evil" is actually a distortion of the New Testament verse from 1 Timothy, "the love of money is the root of all evil."

I Poverty and charity in the pre-modern world

1 This classification derives from the work of E. A. Wrigley, who posits three forms of economies: organic, advanced organic, and mineral-based energy. Each of these will figure prominently in the chapters that follow and will be explained in turn.

2 According to some historians, the European Marriage Pattern represented a strategy among aging parents to forestall their own economic insecurity as well. Fearing that they might not fare well after relinquishing control of their assets to their own children, many parents sought to postpone the potential poverty of old age by preserving their land tenure for as long as they could, making it more difficult for their children to establish their own independent households.

2 Poverty in the emerging global economy

1 Widespread pauperization of indigenous populations also occurred in new European colonies where commercial agriculture and world trade were not necessarily as important as in Latin America. In North America, for example, English settlers frequently expropriated the best hunting grounds for their own needs; in South Africa, Dutch settlers devastated the livelihood of Khoi herdsmen by denying them access to grazing land. In a process far more common in the nineteenth century, and thus discussed in greater detail in Chapter 4, such expropriations forced these indigenous groups either to migrate or to become wage labor.

2 It is that adventurousness and innovation that some Chinese historians often cite as the main difference between China's economic growth during this period and Europe's capitalist development. In China, the absence of new credit structures, impersonal managerial strategies, and legal guarantees for private enterprise indicate the lack of certain fundamental ingredients of capitalism.

3 Innovations in early modern poor relief

1 The few colonies where Europeans settled and attempted to relocate their home institutions, like Latin America and South Africa, are the principal exceptions to this. These establishments and programs had limited impacts, however, and typically followed European models, including the innovations and experiments discussed in this chapter.

4   Industrialization, imperialism, and world poverty, 1750–1945

1   While Japan's industrialization and imperialist endeavors add a slight wrinkle to this image, they too explained their economic success and the subsequent justification for exploiting their neighbors in Social Darwnist terms that privileged race and ethnicity.

Index

able-bodied poor: and begging 30, 34; excluded from relief 28, 83, 88, 90; relief for 31–32, 46, 53, 89; as a threat 50, 55, 79; as undeserving 40, 49, 54, 78–79
absolute poverty 4–5, 17, 111
Africa *See* East Africa; South Africa; sub-Saharan Africa; West Africa
agricultural productivity 16–17, 20–22, 34, 58, 60, 72, 97, 100
al-Ghazzali 27, 29–30
alienation from land 59, 68, 90, 99–100
almsgiving 27–30, 82
Americas 38, 46, 75 *See also* Latin America; United States
Amerindians 39–40
Appalachia 1–2
Argentina 68–69, 99, 102
Asia 35, 95, 97, 99, 112; Central 21; East 115; Southeast 99

benefactors 28, 31, 51, 78, 110
Brazil 39, 71, 97–98, 102, 113
Britain 57, 59, 65, 82, 85–86, 91, 104–5, 110 *See also* England
British colonies 39, 69, 89
Buddhism 26–28, 30–31
bureaucracies 37, 40, 60, 82–83, 87, 97

capitalism 41–43, 49–51, 55, 58, 60–61, 64–68, 82, 97, 102
cash crops 40–41, 43, 58, 71
Catholicism 26, 29, 31, 52, 77, 103
charitable organizations 83–84
charity 25–30, 48, 50–52, 77–78, 80, 82–83, 90
charity workshops 54–55
childcare 63–64, 88, 105

children 32, 63, 74–75, 84, 87, 91, 98–99, 111–12
Children's Protection Society 90
China 35, 69, 111; agriculture 16–18, 21, 72–73, 96, 101; foreign loans 67–68, 74; granaries 31–33, 48; makeshift economy 90–91; population 37, 41; silver 37–38, 44, 115
Christian missionaries 77–78, 90
Christianity 26–29, 31, 50
coercive labor practices 37, 39, 70, 113
Cold War 95, 97, 100, 105, 110, 113
collectivization 66, 96, 101
colonialism 57, 68–69, 75, 79, 85, 93, 96, 105
colonization 38, 113–15
commercial agriculture 21–22, 43, 52, 69, 99
common boxes 52–53
Communist Bloc 105, 112
community self-help 31–33, 43, 49, 90–93, 112
competition: in commerce 33, 42, 44, 62, 72, 81, 100, 102, 107; for housing 61; for jobs 23, 45, 50, 70
compulsory contributory schemes 85–86
Confucianism 79, 81
conjunctural poverty: causes 20–21, 25, 41, 43, 46, 59, 64–66, 70–71, 74–75, 98; relief 28, 50–51, 53, 78–79, 85, 89, 107
consumer markets 40, 58, 97
consumerism 58, 62–63, 74
corruption 97, 110
cottage industries 41–42, 72
criminalization of vagrancy 30, 55, 82–83
crisis poor 10, 25, 98
cultural diversity 15–16

debt: individual 28–30, 37, 44, 46, 71–75, 91; national 1, 3, 68, 70–71, 96, 99, 102, 108, 110, 113
decolonization 95, 98, 115–16
dependence on labor 42, 58
dependence on markets 43, 58–59, 69, 71, 74, 95, 99, 113–14
depopulation 68, 87
depressions 64–66, 71, 74, 80, 86, 89, 92, 96
deserving poor 27–29, 34, 49–53, 78–79, 83
destitution 10, 18, 31, 50–51, 53, 85, 89, 98
devaluation of currency 44, 72
development 45, 96, 100–101, 106–8, 110–11, 114–15
Development Assistance Committee (DAC) 109–12
disasters, natural 16–18, 23, 79, 98, 114
disease 23–24, 38, 61, 109
distribution 17, 31, 58, 95
drought 45, 113–14

East Africa 68, 71
economic crises 96, 98, 108
economic growth 22, 70, 103
economic sustainability 104, 106–7, 109, 112, 114
economy of makeshifts 42–44, 46, 55, 70, 90–92, 112
education 55, 83, 96, 98–99, 101, 103, 109
egalitarianism 50, 81, 98, 103
Egypt 8, 57, 68, 82–84, 100, 110
elderly 10, 18, 23, 26, 31, 39, 51, 74, 98, 111–12
eligibility for relief 29, 53, 79, 89, 92, 107
elites 6, 15, 17, 20, 33–34, 37, 40, 49–51, 63, 68–72
emergency relief 78, 89, 107, 111
England 23–24, 37, 52–54, 61, 65, 79, 83
entitlements, systems of 19–20, 36, 41, 58, 68
Escobar, Arturo 115–16
Europe: pre-modern 19, 22–26, 30–33; early modern 35, 37–38, 40–46, 48–49, 51–55; modern 57–64, 66–72, 75, 77–81, 83–90; postwar 98, 100–102, 104–7, 110–11
export-driven economies 70–71, 95
extreme poverty 4–5, 17, 111

factories 41, 59–61
familial support 26, 30, 73, 90–93
famine 17, 45, 58, 66, 79, 89, 96, 111
fertilization, chemical 97, 100
fiscal discipline 102–3
floating exchange systems 96, 108
flooding of markets 69, 71
Flynn, Dennis O. 37–38
food prices 22, 59, 64
food scarcity 17, 23, 58, 88
food security 97, 109, 111
foreign loans 68, 71, 102
France 23, 37, 44, 52–54, 65–67, 82, 84–87, 107
funding of relief 52, 63, 85–86, 89–90, 107–11

gap between poor and rich 70, 95, 98, 111
gender and poverty 11, 46, 63, 74–75, 92, 98 See also women
Germany 50, 61, 65, 82, 85, 88
Giráldez, Arturo 37–38
global trade 35–37, 41, 43–44, 46, 108
globalization 11–12, 94–95, 97, 115–16
grain banks and granaries 19, 31–32, 48, 53–54
grants 38, 100, 105, 107–10
Green Revolution 97, 100
gross domestic products (GDP) 95, 97, 103, 107, 113–14
gross national products (GNP) 5–6, 111–12
guilds 33, 43, 60

harvest failure 23, 25–26, 32, 36, 41, 44, 64, 114
health care 1, 18, 87–89, 96, 103, 109
Heavily Indebted Poor Country Initiative (HIPC) 1, 108, 113
Hinduism 26–27, 30
HIV/AIDS 98, 112–14
hospitals 31, 54–55
housing 61, 66, 70, 74, 86–88, 99
human capabilities approach 6–7
human development 7–8, 109, 112
Human Development Index (HDI) 7–8
Human Poverty Index (HPI) 7–8
humanism 40, 49
hunger 10, 16–20, 26, 38, 46, 97–98, 111

imbalance of trade 67, 99, 101, 113
imperialism 57–59, 67–72, 75, 78, 82, 84–85, 89, 91, 114

import substitution industrialization (ISI) 96–97, 101–2
indentured servitude 63, 70
India 32, 67, 69, 72–73, 95, 97, 100
indigence 40, 44, 46, 49–51, 78, 80, 98–100
individual responsibility 50, 80, 104
industrial capitalism 58, 61, 64, 66, 68
industrialization 13, 55, 57–67, 75, 78, 84–85, 95–97, 100–103, 115
industrialized nations 57, 59, 65, 71, 79–81, 85, 91, 98
inflation 24, 36, 44, 94, 96
informal economies 90–92, 112, 116
infrastructures 94, 100, 110, 114
innovation: relief 48–55, 79, 88–89, 91; scientific and technical 64, 97
institutions for relief 28, 30–31, 33, 51–54
insurance 81–82, 85–86, 89, 91–92
interest rates 53, 71, 88, 102, 106–8
International Bank for Reconstruction and Development (IBRD) 107–8
International Development Association (IDA) 107–8
international finance 65, 95, 107
International Money Fund (IMF) 1, 102, 107–10, 113
internationalization of relief 85, 91, 94, 105–7, 111, 114
investment 24, 64, 70, 72–73, 100, 102–3, 107
irrigation 16, 18, 97
Islam 27, 29–31, 82–83
isolated economies 65–66

Japan 35–36, 38, 57–58, 60–63, 65, 69, 79–82, 89, 109–10, 115
Judaism 26, 28–29

Kenya 71, 112
kinship networks 93, 112

labor, merit of 48, 50–51
labor supply 51, 71–72, 83
land alienation 59, 68, 90, 99–100
land availability 20–23, 33, 50, 69, 71, 96
landless laborers 22, 44, 100, 106
landlords 23, 41, 43, 72–73
Latin America 36–41, 68–69, 71, 90–92, 95–97, 99, 101–3, 108, 115
leisure 6, 60, 88
liberalism 42, 80–81
life expectancy 7, 61, 112

literacy 4, 7, 80, 82
living standards 5–6, 10, 62, 66, 88, 92, 105
loans 32, 53, 63, 68, 88, 102, 106–8, 110 See also debt
London 54, 80
long-distance markets 22, 40, 42–43, 65, 69, 80, 95
luxuries 6, 24, 26, 29, 40–41, 60, 73

Magnitogorsk 66–67
makeshift economies 42–44, 46, 55, 70, 90–92, 112
malnutrition 24, 58, 62, 74, 100, 109, 111
manufactured goods 38, 58, 65, 69, 114
manufacturing 37, 41, 45, 59–60, 64, 69, 97
Marcos, Ferdinand 97, 110
market economies 19, 75, 99
married women's labor 62, 87
Marshall Plan 105, 109
mass production 22, 25, 59–60, 67, 74
maternalist welfare 54, 81, 83, 87–89, 92, 105
means-testing 86, 105
mechanization 59–60, 64, 66, 74, 100
media 3, 66, 80–82, 108
Mexico 38, 68–69, 97
microcredit 106, 112
middle classes 37, 59, 62, 64, 80, 82, 84, 97, 99
migration 17, 20–21, 34, 39, 45–46, 51, 72; to cities 49, 52, 61, 65, 68, 70, 100; international 65, 104, 113
Millennium Development Goals 111–12
mineral-based energy economies 59, 65
Ming dynasty 37, 44, 48
mining industry 39, 68, 113
missionaries 77–78, 90
modernization 63, 79, 83, 89–90, 101, 105
monasteries 27–28, 31–32, 52
monetization 19, 22, 25, 59
monti frumentari 53–54
moral reform of poor 48–52, 54–55, 77–78, 83, 86, 104
mortality rates 7, 17, 21, 58, 61, 71, 73, 79, 91, 96, 111, 114
Mozambique 1, 3, 113–14
multilateral agencies 108–10
multinational corporations 71, 95–97
mutual benefit organizations 86, 91, 106

Nairobi 70–71
nationalism 72, 81, 84, 87, 89
neoclassical economics 102, 104
neocolonial economies 71, 96
new poor 99, 103
New World crops 36–37, 44–46
non-government organizations (NGO) 106–9
non-industrialized nations 67, 105
Norway 110–11

Official Development Assistance (ODA)
    109–12, 115–16
organic economies 20, 23, 41, 59, 64
organizations for relief 1–2, 12, 83–84, 86,
    90–91, 106–10, 113
orphans 18, 31, 54
Orshansky scale 4–5
Ottoman empire 44, 49, 67–69, 71
outdoor relief programs 51, 53, 55
overcrowding 61, 66, 70, 74, 99
overpopulation 21, 23, 41, 72, 99
overproduction 65, 71

Paris 61, 66–67, 84
patronage 29, 31, 78, 82–83, 90
peasants 43–44, 46, 49–50, 52, 59, 68, 71–
    73, 90, 96, 99–100
pensions 85–86, 91
Peru 38–39
Philippines 97, 110
plague 23–24
plantation economy 36, 39, 41, 68–69, 101,
    113
political in/stability 36–37, 40, 68, 102,
    105, 114
political threat from poverty 50, 63, 81
politicization of relief 31, 79–80, 82–84,
    87–89, 92, 104–6, 110
poor laws 52, 78–79
poor rates 52–53
population: control 61, 80, 101; decrease 24,
    39, 44–45; density 43, 61; increase 21–
    23, 36–37, 41, 44, 46, 58, 70, 100, 114
populist governments 96, 102
Portugal 37–38, 40, 113–14
postwar recovery 94, 99–100, 105
poverty: attitudes towards 9, 77–79, 94, 100–
    104; definitions 2, 4–11, 16, 26, 30, 58
prevention of poverty 28, 30–33, 48, 54–55,
    79–80, 85, 92, 94, 97, 105
prices: control 33, 69, 102; falling 24, 59,
    65; rising 22–24, 44, 46, 64, 66

private charity 16, 28, 30–31, 78, 80, 83–
    84, 86, 88–90, 107
private property 42, 49–50, 101, 103
productivity 16, 20–21, 60, 70, 72, 100–
    102
profit motive 33, 41–42, 73
proletariat 59, 70
prostitution 43, 54
Protestant values 49–50, 52
public benefit organizations 106–7
public health measures 86–87
public pressure 43, 82, 84, 89, 110
public works schemes 53–55, 69, 89

Qin dynasty 20–21
Qing dynasty 48, 68

race 36, 39–40, 68, 75, 89–90, 92–93, 98–
    99, 104, 111–13
railroads 65–66, 69, 113
Rapshuis 48, 51, 54
rationalization of relief 52–54
raw materials 37, 57, 67, 70–71, 96, 99,
    101, 113–14
recessions 59–60, 64–65
redistribution of resources 28–29, 50, 86
Reformation 49–50
reformers 79–82, 84, 86
relative poverty 5–6, 40, 58, 74, 79, 91, 97,
    111
Relief and Protection Law (Japan) 88–89
relief of poverty: premodern 14, 28–34; early
    modern 48–49, 51–55; modern 73, 77–
    80, 82–86, 88–91; postwar 94, 100,
    104–5, 107–9, 111, 113–14
religion and charity 26–31, 82–83
renunciation of property 26–27
replaceability of workers 60–61
research, difficulties of 8–9, 15–16
resource allocation 19–22, 33, 59, 114
respectability 49, 62, 80
restructuring of economies 67–71
Roman empire 20–22
rural poverty 19–20, 23, 33, 43, 51–52, 62,
    70, 92, 106
Russia 37, 66, 82–84, 115

salvation through good works 28, 50, 78
samurai 63, 80
sanitation 61, 66, 74, 86, 109
saturation of markets 64, 102
schools 32, 54

Schweitzer, Albert 77–79, 85
science 50, 78–79, 81, 83, 97
Scott, John 66–67
secularization of relief 48–49, 52, 55, 78, 90
self-help 33, 80, 91, 106
self-identification as poor 26, 99
serfdom 41, 43
service sector 60, 74, 98–99
shame-faced poor 28–30, 40, 51, 62
sharecroppers 68, 71–73, 75
shortages 41, 66, 88, 92, 96
silk trade 41, 44, 63, 69
silver 36–38, 41–42, 44, 72, 115
slavery 32, 35–36, 39–41, 44–46, 58, 113–14
small businesses 62, 73, 106
smallholders 43, 68, 71–73
social control 34, 51, 103
Social Darwinism 81, 87
social exclusion 2, 8, 58, 62, 95, 98, 105
social insurance 81–82, 85–86, 89, 91–92
social mobility 51, 63
social reproduction 87, 89, 105 *See also*
    maternalist welfare
Social Services Division (Colonial Office,
    British empire) 89
social status 20, 22, 25, 30, 40, 62–63, 103
social unrest 23–24, 51, 89
social welfare 58, 79, 82, 85–86, 88–89, 91–
    92, 98, 104–5
socialism 81–82, 103, 114
Society of Egyptian Ladies' Awakening 83–84
sources 9, 13–15
South Africa 68, 71, 89–90, 93, 113
South Korea 97–98
Soviet Union 65–67, 74, 79, 88, 92, 98–99,
    101, 103
Spain 37–40, 52
standardization of aid 82–83, 89
starvation 3, 5, 17, 19, 25, 40, 79, 96
state social welfare 79, 81–85, 87, 89–90, 96
state subsidies 54, 86, 88–89, 91, 99, 110
state-planned economies 88, 101
state-run institutions for relief 30, 48, 55
stigmatization of poor 40, 48–52, 54–55,
    78–79, 82
strangers, charity for 30–31
strikes 81–82
structural adjustment 102–3, 108
structural poverty: premodern 17, 20–22,
    25; early modern 39, 43, 46, 50–51, 53;
    modern 58–59, 62, 64, 66, 70, 73, 75,
    79–80; postwar 95, 98–99

subdivision of land 23, 43
sub-Saharan Africa 75, 99, 112; hunger 96–
    97; imperialism 67–71; makeshift
    economy 91–92; missionaries 77, 79, 90;
    population 37, 46; slave trade 35, 44–45
subsistence farming 41, 58, 68, 95
sugar trade 35, 39–40
supply and demand 42, 58, 65–66, 92
susceptibility 19, 22, 24, 36, 42, 64
sustainable development 104, 106–7, 109,
    112, 114
Sweden 88, 105

tariffs 69, 73, 102
taxes 20, 23, 29–32, 41, 52, 60, 68, 71, 86,
    96
technology 16, 65, 67, 79, 81, 98
textile industry 22–24, 42–43, 51, 63, 65,
    69–70, 73, 95
trade imbalance 67, 99, 101, 113
trade, long-distance 22, 40, 42–43, 65, 69,
    80, 95
transportation 19, 22, 58–59, 61, 65–66,
    69, 79, 110
Turkey 72, 79, 82, 89–90

Uganda 102–3
unemployment 1, 23, 54, 58, 64–65, 71, 86,
    89, 92, 94–95, 99
unions 60, 87
United Nations (UN) 105, 107–8, 110–12
United Nations Children's Fund (UNICEF)
    12, 109
United Nations Development Programme
    (UNDP) 7–9, 109
United States: early modern 39; modern 57,
    60–61, 65, 75, 80–82, 85–87, 93;
    postwar 1–3, 97–98, 102, 104–5, 109–
    10, 115
urban crafts/markets 64, 69, 72–73
urban poverty 19–20, 33, 43, 51–52, 62,
    70, 92, 109
urbanization 21–22, 59, 61, 99, 112

vagrancy 34, 49, 54–55; criminalized 30,
    48, 52–53, 82–83
voluntary poverty 26–27
vulnerability to poverty 10, 43, 46, 58, 60,
    62–64, 70, 78, 114

wage laborers 43, 46, 51, 58, 60–62, 68, 71,
    74, 80

wages: control 33, 61, 65, 70, 79–80, 88;
   differentials 63, 75; increase 24, 59; low
   90, 95, 99; reduction 23, 43, 66
waqf (endowments) 31–32, 49
war 18, 23, 44–45, 59, 96, 98, 113–14
water 2, 4–5, 8, 18, 20, 61, 66, 99
welfare state 79, 85, 88, 91, 96, 104, 115
West Africa 35, 45, 69
West Indies 89
Western hegemony 114, 116
white collar workers 62
Winstanley, Gerard 50
women: in education 2, 83; in the family 2,
   19, 26, 33, 46, 85, 88; in work 43, 46,
   51, 62–64, 70, 75, 87, 91–92, 99, 106

work programs 53–55, 69, 89
workforce reduction 64, 71
workhouses 51, 54–55, 80
working poor 55, 98
World Bank 1, 5, 7, 12, 100, 102, 107–10,
   113
world economy 36–46, 57, 59, 65, 69, 73,
   114–15
World Health Organization (WHO) 109
World War I aftermath 65, 82, 88, 90
World War II aftermath 94–95, 100–101

zakat (alms tax) 29–30
Zhou dynasty 20–21
Zhu Xi 31–32

Routledge History

The United States in World History
Edward J. Davies II

In this concise, accessible introductory survey of the history of the United States from 1790 to the present day, Edward J. Davies examines key themes in the evolution of America from colonial rule to international supremacy.

Focusing particularly on those currents within US history that have influenced the rest of the world, the book is neatly divided into three parts, which examine the Atlantic world, 1700–1800, the US and the industrial world, and the emergence of America as a global power. *The United States in World History* explores such key issues as:

- the dynamics of the British Atlantic community;
- the American revolution;
- the impact of industrialization on the US;
- the expansion of US consumer and cultural industries, the Cold War, and its implications for the US.

Part of our successful *Themes in World History* series, *The United States in World History* presents a new way of examining the United States, and reveals how concepts that originated in American's definition of itself as a nation - concepts such as capitalism, republicanism and race - have had supranational impact across the world.

ISBN10: 0-415-27529-6 (hbk)
ISBN10: 0-415-27530-X (pbk)
ISBN10: 0-203-08621-X (ebk)

ISBN13: 978-0-415-27529-3 (hbk)
ISBN13: 978-0-415-27530-9 (pbk)
ISBN13: 978-0-203-08621-6 (ebk)

Available at all good bookshops
For ordering and further information please visit:
www.routledge.com

Routledge History

Gender in World History

2nd Edition

Peter N. Stearns

'A comparative history of immense ambition ... [It] will be profitably consulted by gender historians. It successfully demonstrates that gender is a historical construct that is rebuilt by each generation and varies from culture to culture.'

Journal of Contemporary History

From classical times to the twenty-first century, *Gender in World History* is a fascinating exploration of what happens to established ideas about men and women, and their roles, when different cultural systems come into contact. This book breaks new ground to facilitate a consistent approach to gender in a world history context.

This second edition is completely updated, including:

- expanded introductions to each chronological section;
- extensive discussion of the twentieth century bringing it right up to date;
- new chapters on international influences in the first half of the twentieth century and globilization in the latter part of the twentieth century;
- engagement with the recent work done on gender history and theory.

Coming right up to the present day, *Gender in World History* is essential reading for students of world history.

ISBN10: 0-415-39588-7 (hbk)
ISBN10: 0-415-39589-5 (pbk)
ISBN10: 0-203-96989-8 (ebk)

ISBN13: 978-0-415-39588-5 (hbk)
ISBN13: 978-0-415-39589-2 (pbk)
ISBN13: 978-0-203-96989-2 (ebk)

Available at all good bookshops
For ordering and further information please visit:
www.routledge.com

Routledge History

Migration in World History
Patrick Manning

From the spread of Homo sapiens onward, migration has been a major factor in human development. This wide-ranging survey traces the connections among regions brought about by the movements of people, diseases, crops, technology and ideas.

Drawing on examples from a wide range of geographical regions and thematic areas, Manning presents a useful overview, including:

- earliest human migrations and the first domestication of major plants and animals;
- the rise and spread of major language groups such as Indo-European, Afro-Asiatic, Niger-Congo, Indo-Pacific, Sino-Tibetan, Altaic, and Amerindian;
- trade patterns including the early Silk Road and maritime trade in the Mediterranean and Indian Ocean;
- the increasing impact of maritime and overland migrations on areas of life such as religion and family;
- the effect of migration on empire and industry between 1700 and 1900;
- the resurgence of migration in the later twentieth century, including movement to cities, refugees and diasporas.

ISBN10: 0-415-31148-9 (hbk)
ISBN10: 0-415-31147-0 (pbk)

ISBN13: 978-0-415-31148-9 (hbk)
ISBN13: 978-0-415-31147-2 (pbk)

Routledge History

Childhood in World History

Peter N. Stearns

Childhood exists in all societies, though there is huge variation in the way it is socially constructed across time and place. Studying childhood historically greatly advances our understanding of what childhood is about and a world history focus permits some of the broadest questions to be asked.

In *Childhood in World History* Peter N. Stearns focuses on childhood in several ways:

- childhood across change - the shift from hunting and gathering to an agricultural society and the impact of civilization and the emergence of major religions;
- new and old debates about the distinctive features of Western childhood, including child labour;
- the emergence of a modern, industrial pattern of childhood in the West, Japan and communist societies, including a focus on education and economic dependence;
- globalization and the spread of child-centred consumerism.

This historical perspective highlights the gains but also the divisions and losses for children across the millennia.

ISBN10: 0-415-35232-0 (hbk)
ISBN10: 0-415-35233-9 (pbk)
ISBN10: 0-203-69893-2 (ebk)

ISBN13: 978-0-415-35232-1 (hbk)
ISBN13: 978-0-415-35233-8 (pbk)
ISBN13: 978-0-203-69893-8 (ebk)

Routledge History

Religion in World History
John C. Super and Briane K. Turley

Individuals and groups have long found identity and meaning through religion and its collective expression. In *Religion and World History*, John C. Super and Briane K. Turley examine the value of religion for interpreting the human experience in the past and present. This study explores those elements of religion that best connect it with cultural and political dynamics that have influenced history.

Working within this general framework, Super and Turley bring out three unifying themes:

- the relationship between formal and informal religious beliefs, how these change through time, and how they are reflected in different cultures;
- the relationship between church and state, from theocracies to the repression of religion;
- the ongoing search for spiritual certainty, and the consequent splintering of core religious beliefs and the development of new ones.

The book's unique approach helps the reader grasp the many and complex ways that religion acts upon and reacts to broader global processes.

ISBN10: 0-415-31457-7 (hbk)
ISBN10: 0-415-31458-5 (pbk)
ISBN10: 0-203-96958-8 (ebk)

ISBN13: 978-0-415-31457-2 (hbk)
ISBN13: 978-0-415-31458-9 (pbk)
ISBN13: 978-0-203-96958-8 (ebk)

Available at all good bookshops
For ordering and further information please visit:
www.routledge.com